GEORGIA TRAVEL GUIDE 2020

MARIAM GUDZUADZE

OPPIAN

Published by Oppian Press
Helsinki, Finland

ISBN 978-951-877-138-1

GENERAL INFORMATION
ABOUT GEORGIA

GEOGRAPHY AND DEMOGRAPHICS

Georgia – also referred to as Sakartvelo in Georgian – is situated on the border of Western Asia and Eastern Europe. The country is bounded by the Black Sea to the west, by Russia to the north, by Turkey and Armenia to the south, and by Azerbaijan to the east and southeast. An essential part of Georgian land is situated in the South Caucasus while remaining parts of the country are located in the North Caucasus.

Despite the country's small area, Georgia is appreciated for its diverse variety of topography. It is considered as one of the most impressive countries in the Caucasus region. Georgia comprises mountainous areas and ski resorts full of nomadic sheepherders, as well as cities and beach areas best night clubs.

According to the data retrieved in 2018, total population of Georgia (excluding Abkhazia and South Ossetia) is approximately 3,729,000. Ethnic makeup of Georgia is the following: 86.8% Georgians (Kartvelebi), 6.3% Azerbaijanis, 4.5% Armenians, 0.7% Russians, 0.4% Ossetians, 0.3% Yazidis, 0.1% Kurds, 0.2% Caucasus Greeks, 0.2% Ukrainians, 0.2% Abkhazians, 0.1% Assyrians, 0.1% Jews, 0.4% other.

HISTORY

Evidence of the earliest occupation of the territory of the present-day Georgia date back to about 1.8 million years ago (from excavations of Dmanisi in the southeastern part of the country). The latest agricultural Neolithic occupation dates back to 6000-5000 BC (Shulaveri-Shomu culture). Moreover, early metallurgy started during the 6th millennium BC.

Since the history of Georgia is quite comprehensive, essential periods for the country will be briefly discussed throughout the next several paragraphs.

In classical times, there were to major kingdoms: Colchis in the west (legendary home of the Golden Fleece and the site of Greek colonies) and Kartli in the east and south (also referred to es Iveria or Iberia), including part of the territories of modern Turkey and Armenia.

There have been several vital stages, the first of which can be said to be the Golden Age. Davit Aghmashenebeli (Davit the Builder) made Georgia the significant Caucasian power and a center of Christian culture and learning after he defeated the Seljuk Turks ad Didgori in 1122. He recaptured nearby Tbilisi and made it the capital city. Georgia reached its zenith under Davit's great-granddaughter Tamar Mepe (King Tamar). Her writ extended over much of present-day Azerbaijan and Armenia, as well as included parts of Turkey and southern Russia.

The golden age ended when the Mongols arrived in the country in the 1220s. Even though King Giorgi Brtskinvale (Giorgi the Brilliant) shook off the Mongol yoke, Mongols were followed by the Central Asian destroyer Timur (Tamerlane) who attacked the country eight times (from 1386 to 1403). As a result, Georgia split into four kingdoms: Kartli and Kakheti in the east, Imereti in the northwest and Samtskhe in the southwest. Starting from the early 16th century for over two centuries, the Ottoman Turks and the Persian Safavid Empire were vying for the control of the Transcaucasus region. Consequently, western Georgia fell under Turkish control while the eastern part under the Persians. From 1762, both kingdoms were ruled by Erekle II as a semi-independent state.

Russian troops crossed the Caucasus in 1770 for the first time to assist Imereti's liberation from the Turks. Erekle II accepted Christian Russians, but they had to protect the country against Muslim enemies. Unfortunately, Russia continued to annex all Georgia kingdoms and princedoms during the 19th century. Thus, Turkish rulers were replaced by Russian military governors.

Georgia gained brief independence from 1918 to 1921, but

the country was still invaded by the Red Army and was incorporated into the Soviet Union in 1922. Georgia suffered from the terror unleashed by Joseph Stalin (as everywhere else in the USSR). After Stalin's death in 1953, the country began to enjoy high-quality life (the 1960s and 1970s).

On April 9th in 1991, Georgia (anti-Communist government led by the nationalist intellectual Zviad Gamsakhurdia) was declared as independent from the USSR. But the dream turned into a nightmare. The next president of the country was Eduard Shevardnadze which strengthened Georgia's reputation abroad; Though, devastating internal conflicts continue to worsen. In 1993 Georgia suffered from a comprehensive defeat in Abkhazia as a consequent of which 250,000 Georgians forcibly left their homes.

The next important event in Georgian history was the Rose Revolution in 2003 which was a result of severely flawed parliamentary elections. The mass protest movement turned into a bloodless coup. The protestors remained in front of the parliament until Shevardnadze resigned.

As a result of the Russo-Georgian war on August 7-12 in 2008, Georgia lost control over the territories of Abkhazia and former South Ossetia. Currently, Abkhazia and South Ossetia are considered as Russian-occupied territories for Georgians. In 2011, these territories were also acknowledged by the European Parliament to be occupied by Russia.

RELIGION

Georgia adopted Christianity as the official state religion in 326CE. It was the second country in the world to take Christianity (after Armenia). According to the legend, the Mother of God had to spread the doctrine of Christ in new lands. Georgia is considered to be the chosen country of the Mother of God who is considered as the patroness of the country.

Even though the Mother of God herself was left in Jerusalem,

Saint Andrew the Apostle went to Georgia with the Vernicle Image of the Mother of God. The Apostle visited many cities and villages preaching the Gospel. The Apostle left the icon of the Virgin Mary in the town of Atskuri. For that reason, there are celebrations in honor of the Atskuri icon of the Mother of God on August 15th and 28th.

When King Mirian and Queen Nana of Kartli identified Christianity as their religion in the early 4th century, Georgia became the second country to adopt the Christian faith. By the 4th century, Christianity was firmly spread in Georgia, but huge threats were coming from foreign enemies, including but not limited to the Persians, Arabs, Turks, and Mongols. Lots of people were martyred since they refused to obey enemies and change religion. Famous martyrs include King Archil (6th century), Princes David and Konstantin Mkheidze (8th century), King Demetre II (13th century, killed by the Mongols), King Luarsab II (17th century, killed by the Persians), and Queen Ketevani (17th century, tortured to death by the Persians).

Since Georgia was part of the Russian Empire in the early 19th century, the Georgian Orthodox Church was forcibly integrated into the Russian Orthodox Church. After the gain of independence in 1917, the Independent Georgian Orthodox Church was reestablished. Moreover, Archbishop of Mtskheta and Tbilisi has been Ilia II since 1977.

4

LANGUAGE

The official language of Georgia is Georgian, which is a Kartvelian language spoken by Georgians. The writing system of the language is called the Georgian script.

The Georgian language is one of the oldest throughout the world. It has its own alphabet which is unique and differs dramatically from any other alphabet. According to Georgian scholars, the creation of the Georgian script is linked to King Parnavaz who ruled in the 3rd century BC. For that reason, it is considered that the Georgian script dates back to the 3rd century BC.

As it was already mentioned above, Georgian language has its own alphabet which has undergone three stages of evolvement: Asomtavruli, Nuskhakhutsuri, and Mkhedruli (used today having 33 letters).

Even though several regional subgroups of Georgia, including Svans, Mingrelians, and the Laz speak other Kartvelian languages, Georgian is still the literary language for the entire country.

There are diverse dialects of Georgian from various regions of the country, including Imereti, Racha-Lechkhumi, Guria, Adjara, Imerkhevi (Turkey), Kartli, Kakheti, Saingilo (Azerbaijan), Khevsureti, Khevi, Pshavi, Fereydan (Iran), Mtiuleti, and

Meskheti. For that reason, any tourist will notice that even though Georgians speak the same language, they pronounce each and every word differently depending on the region they represent.

5

GEORGIAN CUISINE

Georgian cuisine is quite diverse and comprehensive. Some of the most popular examples corresponding to the specific region of the country are provided in the table below:

REGIONAL CUISINE

Abkhazia

Abkhazura – fried spicy meatballs;

Abkhazia-style roasted chicken with "ajika" sauce.

Samegrelo

Elarji – variety of Ghomi (traditional dish made with corn-meal) with cheese;

Gebzhalia – soft cheese rolls stuffed with curd cheese and mint;

Ajika – hot and spicy sauce made from red pepper, garlic, and dried spices.

Svaneti

Kubdari – meat-filled pastry;

Svanuri Salt – traditional spicy salt.

Racha

Lobiani – bean-filled pastry;

Shkmeruli – fried chicken in creamy garlic sauce.

Adjara

Adjaruli Khachapuri – boat-shaped Georgian cheese bread in shape with partially cooked egg and chunk of butter;

Achma – type of Khachapuri (Georgian cheese bread), often comparet to lasagna for its texture and appearance;

Borano – made of Adjarian cheese and salted butter.

Imereti

Imeruli Khachapuri – most famous and classical type of Khachapuri;

Various types of pkhali (Georgian appetizier made with herbs and walnuts).

Kakheti

Mtsvadi – Georgian barbeque;

Churchkhela – Georgian candy made of grape must, flour, and walnuts.

Samtskhe-Javakheti

Tatarberak – traditional dish made with tiny pieces of dough boiled and served with the sauce of melted butter and fried onion.

Moreover, the most popular Georgian cuisine is Khinkali, which is generally meat-filled Georgian dumpling. Various regions of Georgia make Khinkali with different techniques and fillings.

6

SAFETY AND SECURITY

Obviously, cases of petty thefts, robbery, and mugging are reported in Georgia, but the crime rate of the country is one of the lowest in Europe which means that it is quite safe to travel to Georgia at any time of the year. Many police officers are patrolling the steers during the day and even at night.

Lots of tourists have reported that they have never noticed any suspicious behavior while taking pictures with quite an expensive camera in Georgia. Moreover, the fact that people are very lovely and helpful makes the place even safer since Georgians are always happy to support and assist tourists in case of any need.

But still, there are things that you should consider for your safe travel to Georgia. Several essential tips and tricks for visitors of Georgia will be discussed below under several sections.

- <u>Crime</u> – even though crime levels are quite low in Georgia, you should still exercise particular caution.
- Be careful in areas frequently visited by tourists (a few incidents of pickpocketing involving foreigners have been reported);
- Keep your mobile phone charged and with you at all times;
- If you are the victim of an attempted assault,

discrimination or feel threatened, dial "112" to contact the needed emergency service.

- Traveling near Abkhazia and South Ossetia
- Take care not to cross the Administrative Boundary Lines with Abkhazia and South Ossetia inadvertently as you risk arrest;
- Hire a professional guide if you plan to hike close to these boundary lines;
- Do not enter Georgia from Russia via South Ossetia or Abkhazia (you may face criminal prosecution);
- Consult FCO Travel Advice for Russia in case if you are considering to travel to Russia via the land borders with the Russian Federation;
- Be cautious in areas along the Administrative Boundary Lines with South Ossetia, Abkhazia, and near the border with Azerbaijan (Red Bridge area in particular). There is some risk from unexploded ordnance.
- Local Travel
- Take extra precautions after dark in unfamiliar areas (as you would in your hometown);
- Street lighting far from the main roads might be weak and pavements uneven. Have your phone charged to use the flashlight if needed.
- Road Travel
- Driving is on the right;
- Speed limit in towns and cities is 60 km/h (unless indicated);
- Speed limit in other areas is 80 km/h (unless indicated);
- Zero tolerance policy towards drunk drivers;
- Wearing seat belts in the front seats is compulsory;
- Children under the age of 12 must sit in the back seat of a car.
- Children under the age of 7 must sit in child safety seats;
- Make sure your vehicle is suitably equipped if you are

traveling outside of Tbilisi since landslides are frequent during the heavy rain or wind.

- <u>Transportation</u>
- Public transportation is quite safe and efficient with fixed prices;
- Try to avoid local taxis, since they try to charge higher rates when they see a foreigner. Moreover, it is safer to order a taxi through an app to get a reasonable price for your trip as well as the detailed information about the driver.
- Avoid sitting in the front seat of a taxi. Better rest in the back seat depending on the availability of working seatbelts and space;
- <u>Mountaineering and Extreme Sports</u>
- Take appropriate precautions when skiing;
- The level of emergency response might be limited in mountainous areas during skiing or hiking;
- Georgian authorities are working hard to ensure the proper safety standards since Georgia's winter and adventure sports industry gradually develops.

7

ENTRY REQUIREMENTS

There are different categories of visas that apply to the particular occasion and are dependent on the purpose of an individual's travel (visit, study, work, reside permanently) to Georgia.

There is a simple online application which can help you get the detailed information regarding the type of Georgian Visa that you need (if you need one) to enter/stay in Georgia or transit the territory of Georgia. You can follow the link provided below:

https://bit.ly/2nDf2RW

- Visa-Free Regime

Even though citizens of a foreign country who are willing to enter Georgia typically must obtain a Georgian visa, specific international travelers may still be eligible to travel to Georgia without a permit (in case if they meet the requirements for visa-free travel).

Citizens of 98 countries are allowed to enter/reside/work/study in Georgia without obtaining either a visa or residence permit. Along with that, visa and/or residence permit holders of 50 countries may enter the country without a visa for an appropriate period and under proper conditions.

List of countries whose citizens are allowed to enter Georgia without a visa for 1 full year is provided below:

EU States, Albania, Andorra, Antigua and Barbuda, Argentina, Armenia, Australia, Azerbaijan, Bahamas, Bahrain, Barbados, Belarus, Belize, Bosnia and Herzegovina, Jordan, Botswana, Brazil, British Dependent Territories, British Overseas Territories, Brunei, Canada, Chile (90/180 days), Colombia, Costa Rica, Denmark Territories, Dominican Republic, Ecuador, El Salvador, French Republic Territories, Holy See, Honduras, Iceland, Iran (45 days), Israel Japan, Kazakhstan, Kuwait, Kyrgyzstan, Lebanon, Liechtenstein, Malaysia, Mauritius, Mexico, Moldova, Monaco, Montenegro, Netherlands Territories, New Zealand, Norway, Oman, Panama, Qatar, Russia, Saint Vincent and Grenadines, San Marino, Saudi Arabia, Serbia, Seychelles, Singapore, South Africa, South Korea, Switzerland, Tajikistan, Thailand, Turkey, Turkmenistan, Ukraine, United Arab Emirates, United States of America, Uruguay (90 days), Uzbekistan.

Along with the countries provided above, holders of diplomatic or official/service passports of China, Egypt, Guyana, India, Shri Lanka, Indonesia, and Peru are allowed to enter and stay in Georgia without a visa.

- <u>Visa Regime</u>

Citizens of the countries which are not in the list of the visa-free regime countries must obtain a visa according to the purpose of their visit to Georgia. Georgian visa categories are the following:
- Diplomatic (A)
- Special (B)
- Ordinary (C)
- Immigration (D)
- Transit (T)

There are several options to apply for Georgian visa information regarding which is provided below:

- <u>E-Visa Portal</u> – most straightforward way to get permit of entry into and travel within Georgia in case of a short stay. There is no need to visit the Georgian Embassy or Consular office for the short-term visa.
- You can follow the link below for further details regarding the procedure: https://bit.ly/1COv1w5
- <u>E-Application System</u> – this system makes it possible to apply for any category of visa. Through the system one can submit an online application for booking time for submission of visa application at the appropriate consular office.
- You can follow the link below for further details regarding the procedure: https://bit.ly/2pw7FKu

Time Zone

Time Zone in Georgia's every region is GMT+4 (or UTC+4)

8

CURRENCY AND BANKS

The currency of Georgia is the Georgian Lari or simply referred to as Lari. Considering the ISO 4217 standard, Lari is abbreviated as GEL.

1 Lari or 1 GEL = 100 Tetri
Coins include the following:

- 1 Tetri- 20 Tetri
- 2 Tetri- 50 Tetri
- 5 Tetri- 1 Lari(was printed as a banknote until 2006)
- 10 Tetri- 2 Lari (was printed as a banknote until 2006)

Banknotes include the following:

- 5 Lari- 100 Lari
- 10 Lari- 200 Lari
- 20 Lari- 500 Lari (has never been officially released)
- 50 Lari

1 Georgian Lari is approximately:

- 1 Lari = 0.34 US Dollar
- 1 Lari = 0.31 Euro
- 1 Lari = 0.27 Pound Sterling

For more accurate currency conversion, you can use the National Bank of Georgia website by following the URL: https://bit.ly/2mm2QCF

You can exchange currencies at any Currency Exchange Point throughout the country. It will not be reasonable to list addresses for every Currency Exchange Point since they are situated on almost every street and are quite noticeable for the eye.

Information about the banks in Georgia is provided below:

TBC Bank
+995 32 227 27 27
www.tbcbank.ge
Bank of Georgia
+995 32 244 44 44
www.bankofgeorgia.ge
Liberty Bank
+995 32 255 55 00
www.libertybank.ge
Basis Bank
+995 32 292 29 22
www.basisbank.ge
VTB Bank
+995 32 224 24 24
www.vtb.ge
Cartu Bank
+995 32 200 80 80
www.cartubank.ge
ProCredit Bank
+995 32 220 22 22
www.procreditbank.ge
Silk Road Bank
+995 32 224 22 22
www.silkroadbank.ge

Ziraat Bank Georgia
+995 32 294 37 04
www.ziraatbank.ge
Isbank Georgia
+995 32 231 05 18
www.isbank.ge
Terabank
+995 32 255 00 00
www.terabank.ge
Halyk Bank
+995 32 224 07 07
www.halykbank.ge
PASHA Bank Georgia
+995 32 226 50 00
www.pashabank.ge
FINCA Bank
+995 32 224 49 49
www.finca.ge
Credo Bank
+995 32 242 42 42
www.credo.ge
International Bank of Azerbaijan Georgia
+995 32 229 22 22
www.ibaz.ge
Public Holidays

DATE: HOLIDAY

January 1
New Year's Day
January 7
Orthodox Christmas
January 19
Orthodox Epiphany/Baptism
March 3
Mother's Day
March 8

Women's Day
April 9
National Unity Day
May 9
Victory Against Fascism Day
May 26
Independence Day
August 28
Mariamoba (Day of the Virgin Mary)
October 14
Svetitskhovloba
November 23
Saint George's Day

*Easter Holidays - Orthodox Good Friday, Orthodox Holy Saturday, Orthodox Easter Sunday, Orthodox Easter Monday – dates are variable

9

PHONE SERVICES

- Country calling code +995
- International calling prefix 00
- Trunk prefix 0
- Destination area code – depends on the region throughout the country
- Mobile network code – depends on the mobile operator

Dial Georgia from Abroad:

+995 – Destination Area Code – Subscriber's Phone Number

+995 – Mobile Network Code – Subscriber's Phone Number

Dial any destination from Georgia:

00 – Destination Country Code – Destination Area Code - Subscriber's Phone Number

00 – Destination Country Code – Mobile Network Code – Subscriber's Phone Number

The landline phone number is usually 6-digit-number. "32" is the area code for Tbilisi. If you want to dial another destination in Georgia, simply use the corresponding area code instead of "32".

Dial Landline Phone: (for instance in Tbilisi)
    XXX XX XX – within Tbilisi
    0 32 XXX XX XX – within Georgia
    +995 32 XX XX XX – from abroad

Mobile phone number is a 9-digit-number. First 3 digits of the number are dependent on the mobile operator. In this instance, "AAA" indicates the prefix of a certain provider.
    Dial Mobile Number:
    AAA XX XX XX – from mobile network, within Georgia
    0 AAA XX XX XX – from a landline phone, within Georgia
    +995 AAA XX XX XX

MOBILE NETWORKS

Three main companies are operating in Georgia and offer GSM sim cards. Moreover, there are two more companies which work only in Abkhazia.

The list of mobile network providers operating throughout the country is shown below:
    Magticom - https://www.magticom.ge/en/home
    Geocell$_{Silknet}$ - https://geocell.ge
    Beeline - https://www.beeline.ge/

The list of the mobile network providers operating only in Abkhazia:
    Aquafon - http://www.aquafon.com/
    A-Mobile - https://www.a-mobile.biz/

TRANSPORTATION

Subway

Subway operates only in Tbilisi. There are 2 subway lines with a total of 23 stations of the Tbilisi Metro Which are the listed below:

Akhmeteli-Varketili LineSaburtalo Line

- Varketili- Station Square 2
- Samgori- Tsereteli
- Isani- Technical University
- 300 Aragveli- Medical University
- Avlabari- Delisi
- Freedom Square- Vazha-Pshavela
- Rustaveli- State University
- Marjanishvili
- Station Square
- Nadzaladevi
- Gotsiridze
- Didube
- Ghrmaghele
- Guramishvili
- Sarajishvili
- Akhmeteli Theatre

- It is quite easy to navigate in the subway. The two stations that are highlighted in green are the stops where you might have to change the train depending on your destination. There are big boards between the 2 train lines where you can check which lane is suitable for you.
- You can get further details by following the website below:
- https://bit.ly/2nD9E12

- City Bus
- Currently, there are city buses of three colors operating in Tbilisi: Dark Green, Dark Blue, and Yellow. Dark Green and Blue buses are entirely new and well-equipped while the yellow ones are somewhat old. It is planned to gradually change all the yellow city buses with the new ones.
- For further information about every route for every bus, you can follow the links provided below:
- https://bit.ly/2krEzfror https://bit.ly/2nD9E12

- Minibus – also referred to as Marshrutka
- Small yellow minibusses operate in all the districts of Tbilisi and in some other regions as well.
- To get more information about the specific route of each minibus, you should follow the website below:
- https://bit.ly/2nD9E12

- Taxi
- There are various local taxi drivers throughout the country, but it is much safer to order a taxi from

multiple apps operating in Georgia. The list of major Taxi operators in Georgia is provided below:

- Yandex Taxi
- Maxim Taxi
- Bolt
- You can download the app of corresponding Taxi operator and order a Taxi at your current location.

- <u>Car Rentals</u>
- You can rent a car within Georgia for a specific period. Several companies offering car rental services are provided below:
- www.larirent.ge
- www.naniko.com
- www.4x4carrental.ge
- www.carsandrooms.ge
- www.race.com.ge
- www.myauto.ge

- <u>Railway</u>
- Georgian railway connects different regions of Georgia. It is a very convenient way of traveling from one place to another. To get farther information about the routes, prices, and different options, follow the website below:
- http://www.railway.ge/

- <u>Airports</u>
- The list of major public airports within the territories of Georgia is provided below:

- - Tbilisi International Airporthttp://www. tbilisiairport.com/
- - Kutaisi International Airporthttp://www. kutaisi.aero/
- - Batumi International Airporthttp://www. batumiairport.com/
- - Mestia Airport
- - Ambrolauri Airporthttps://bit.ly/2nAGQpX
- - Natakhtari Airport

APARTMENT RENTAL WEBSITES

This travel guide provides information regarding specific hotels located in every region of Georgia that are popular and most visited by not only tourists but also the local people. Besides that, there are a lot more hotels, hostels, or rental apartments available for every tourist.

Here is a list of primary websites which are helpful to get more detailed information regarding various accommodation options:

https://www.booking.com/
https://www.airbnb.com/
https://www.dgiurad.ge/
https://ss.ge/en/real-estate
https://livo.ge/
https://myhome.ge/
https://place.ge/
https://home.ge/
https://binebi.info

ONLINE TICKETS

There are various events held throughout the whole year within different regions of Georgia. Even though tickets are usually also sold on the door, it is much more convenient to buy tickets online. In almost all cases, online tickets are a little bit less expensive compared to the ones sold on the door. Moreover, while buying tickets online, you can choose between the seats and purchase the suitable one.

The list of primary websites selling online tickets is provided below:

https://tkt.ge/
https://www.kinoafisha.ge/ (tickets only for movies)
https://eventikz.com/

GAS STATIONS AND EV CHARGERS

Filling up with fuel in Georgia is quite easy and straightforward process. Because gas stations are not self-served, you might have some language barriers with the staff working at a station. Here are some tips that tourists should know in case if they need to fill up the tank.

There are 4 types of gasoline offered: Super (grade 98), Premium (grade 95), Euro Regular (grade 92), and Euro Diesel. Prices are around 1$ per liter and vary, considering the type of gas your car takes.

Most of the service stations throughout the country accept credit cards as well as cash. Be aware that small stations in villages or mountainous regions might only take cash. The currency of payment is in GEL.

Most popular gas stations in Georgia are listed below:

Wissol - http://www.wissol.ge/

Rompetrol - https://www.rompetrol.ge/en/personal

Lukoil - http://lukoil.ge/

Socar - https://socar.ge/en

Gulf - https://gulf.ge/en/home

Frego - http://frego.ge/en/

It is considered that Rompetrol, which is a Romanian company, provides the best quality fuel in Georgia, but the prices are higher compared to other gas stations. On the other hand, Frego is the cheapest gas station. Moreover, you can get cheaper rates in smaller gas stations without brands, but it is not highly recommended.

Electric vehicles are not that common in Georgia, but the number and popularity of such cars among the Georgian people are gradually increasing. You can check the EV charger locations by following the link: https://bit.ly/2kXC590

POSTAL SERVICES

- Georgian Post

The leading national postal operator in Georgia is the Georgian Post.
    Head Office - 2 Station Square, 0100 Tbilisi, Georgia
    Phone Number - +995 32 24 09 09
    E-mail – info@gpost.ge
    Website - https://www.gpost.ge/

- DHL

Another facility that provides postal services is DHL.
Address – 105 Akaki Tsereteli Avenue, 0119 Tbilisi, Georgia
Phone Number - +995 32 269 99 66
Website - https://www.dhl.com/en/ge/country_profile.html

FOOD DELIVERY

Even though there are restaurants that offer their delivery service, there are three major food delivery companies operating in Georgia.

Menu.ge
Website - https://www.menu.ge
Address – 45 Vazha-Pshavela Ave. 0179 Tbilisi, Georgia
Phone Number - +995 32 254 44 44
Mobile App – iOS: https://apple.co/2mQ3I4M
Android: https://bit.ly/2m5n4Cy

Glovo
Website - https://glovoapp.com/en/
Mobile App – iOS: https://apple.co/2nKL7qL
Android: https://bit.ly/2m5Lxrv

Wolt
Website - https://wolt.com/en/geo/
Mobile App – iOS: https://apple.co/2omOe8S
Android: https://bit.ly/2og5GM3

CONSUL-GENERALS, HONORARY CONSULS, AND EMBASSIES

To get the detailed information regarding the Consul-Generals, Honorary Consuls, or Embassies of a particular country in Georgia, follow the link below:

https://bit.ly/2oi5CLP

Important Contacts

Information Call Centre – "118 08"

Public Service Hall (House of Justice) – +995 32 2 405 405; http://psh.gov.ge/

Ministry of Foreign Affairs - +995 32 294 50 00; http://www.mfa.gov.ge/

Tbilisi City Hall - +995 32 272 22 22; http://tbilisi.gov.ge/?lang=en

EMERGENCY NUMBER

There is only one Emergency Number in Georgia that provides any type of urgent service.

Emergency Number – "112"

Website: http://112.gov.ge/

By calling "112" you can get the following services:

- Police
- Ambulance
- Firefighting Crew
- Extreme Situation Management Crew

REGIONS, MUNICIPALITIES, AND CITIES OF GEORGIA

1

TBILISI

Architecture in Old Tbilisi

• Geography and Demographics

Tbilisi, the capital of Georgia, is the largest city of the country
with the area of 726km^2 a population of over 1.5 million. Lying

in Eastern Georgia on both banks of the Mtkvari River (Kura River), Tbilisi serves as an essential transit route for diverse energy and trade projects. The city which is surrounded by mountains on three sides is 380-770 meters above the sea level.

• **Climate and Seasonality**

Climate zone in Tbilisi is either Humid Subtropical Climate (characteristic to Tskneti, Telovani, Didgori, Shindisi, Tabakhmela) or Warm/Hot-Humid Climate with continental influences (Zahesi, Tsinubani, Patara Lilo, Didi Lilo, Okrokana). Summers in the city are hot while winters are moderately cold.

The average annual temperature – 13.3°C.

The coldest month – January (an average temperature of 2.3°C).

The hottest month – July (an average temperature of 24.9°.

Best time to visit Tbilisi is late Spring or early Autumn since the weather during these periods of the year is not too cold, nor too hot.

• **History**

The history of the ancient city, Tbilisi, counts 16 centuries. According to the most wide-spread legend, the present-day area of Tbilisi was covered by forests until 458. The myth states that King Vakhtang I of Iberia, also referred to as Vakhtang Gorgasali, went hunting with a falcon. The falcon caught or injured a pheasant during the hunt as a result of which both, falcon and pheasant, fell into a nearby hot spring. King Vakhtang was so impressed with the scene that he decided to clear the forest and establish a city.

The successor of Vakhtang I, King Dachi of Iberia, moved the capital of Iberia from Mtskheta to Tbilisi.

The name of the city derives from Old Georgian from the

Georgian word *"tbili"* meaning *"warm."* The name was given to the town because of the presence of numerous sulfuric hot springs. Until 1936, the name of the city in most foreign languages was *Tiflis*, while in Georgian it was Tpilisi. The name was later modernized and replaced by *Tbilisi.*

Considering the location of Tbilisi (in the heart of the Caucasus between Europe and Asia), the city has been an object of rivalry among different regions including but not limited to the Roman Empire, Parthia, Sassanid Persia, Arabs, the Byzantine Empire, and the Seljuk Turks. For that reason, Tbilisi was a cosmopolitan city influenced by various rulers.

After heavy fighting with the Seljuks, known as the Battle of Didgori (1121-1122), David IV of Georgia (David Aghmashenebeli) moved his residence from Kutaisi to Tbilisi, making Tbilisi the capital of a unified Georgian State. This era has been known as the Georgian Golden Age, which did not last for more than a century.

After that, Georgia came under Mongol Domination and later vassal territories of Safavid Iran were formed. In the early 19th century, the Russian Empire annexed the Georgian Kingdom of Kartli-Kakheti and Tbilisi became the center of the Tbilisi Governorate. After the Russian Revolution of 1917, Tbilisi gained brief independence and served as a location of the Transcaucasus interim government. In 1921, the Democratic Republic of Georgia was occupied by the Soviet Bolshevik forces from Russia and Tbilisi functioned first as the capital city of the Transcaucasian SFSR and later as the capital of the Georgian Soviet Socialistic Republic. The town witnessed various anti-Russian demonstrations including the April 9 Tragedy.

- **Religion**

The city has always been the home to people from various cultural, religious, and ethnic backgrounds. Even though Tbilisi is predominantly an Eastern Orthodox Christian city, it still comprises the Orthodox church, Catholic church, Gregorian church, Minaret, and Synagogue.

- **Districts**

Tbilisi consists of 10 districts most of which are named after historic quarters of the city. The districts are provided below:

Mtatsminda District

Mtatsminda, Sololaki, Vera, Kiketi, Kojori, Shindisi, Tsavkisi, Tabakhmela

Vake District

Vake, Bagebi, Vazha Pshavela Quarters, Nutsubidze Plateau, Tskneti

Saburtalo District

Delisi, Vedzisi, Vashlijvari, Bakhtrioni, Khiliani, Didi Dighomi, Zurgovana

Krtsanisi District

Kala, Ortachala, Ponichala

Isani District

Avlabari, Navtlughi, Metromsheni, Vazisubani, Eighth Legion

Samgori District

Varketili, Third Array, Orkhevi, Dampalo, Lilo, Lower Samgori

Chughureti District

Chughureti, Kukia, Svanetisubani

Didube District

Didube, Dighomi Massive

Nadzaladevi District

Nadzaladevi, Sanzona, Temka, Lotkini, Old Nadzaladevi

Gldani District

Gldani Massive, Avchala, Mukhiani, Gldanula

- **Sightseeing and Highlights**

Churches and Cathedrals

- *The Holy Trinity Cathedral of Tbilisi (Tsminda Sameba Cathedral)*, also referred to as *Sameba* – main cathedral of the Georgian Orthodox Church located in the historic neighborhood Avlabari in Old Tbilisi. Constructed between 1995 and 2004 to commemorate 1500 years of autocephaly of the Georgian Orthodox Church and 2000 years from the birth of Jesus, it is identified as the third-tallest Eastern Orthodox cathedral in the world and also one of the largest religious building across the globe considering the total area ($3000m^2$).
- While Sameba reflects traditional styles of Georgian church architecture at various historical eras, it has some Byzantine undertones as well. The cathedral comprises nine chapels, each corresponding to a saint (Archangels, John the Baptist, Saint Nino, Saint George, Saint Nicholas, the Twelve Apostles).

- *Mtatsminda Pantheon* - also referred to as *Mtatsminda Pantheon of Writers and Public Figures* – a necropolis which buries some of the most noteworthy writers, scholars, artists, and national heroes. Established in 1929, it is located in the churchyard around Saint David's Church *"Mamadaviti."*
- Officially opened for the centennial celebration of Griboyedov's death in Iran, the Pantheon is administered by the Government of Tbilisi.

- *Anchiskhati Basilica of Saint Mary* – identified as the oldest surviving church in Tbilisi dating from the 6th century. According to the history, the church was built by the King Dachi of Iberia, dedicating to the Virgin Mary. The church was renamed in 1675 when the treasured icon of Jesus Christ was moved to Tbilisi to preserve it from an Ottoman invasion.

- The basilica was rebuilt several times between the 15th and 17th centuries (due to the wars between Georgia and Persians and Turks). Original construction made of blocks of yellow tuff stone was changed by bricks due to the 1958-1964 restoration in celebration of the 1500 years from the foundation of Tbilisi.

- *Kashveti Church of Saint George* – Georgian Orthodox Church located in central Tbilisi on Rustaveli Avenue. The name of the church constructed from 1904 to 1910 comes from the legend from the 6th century according to which a woman accused monk David of Gareja of making her pregnant. David's denial was proven when the woman gave birth to a stone. The place received the name of "Kashveti" (*"kva"* for a *"stone," "shva"* for *"giving birth."*

- *The Sioni Cathedral of the Dormition* – Georgian Orthodox cathedral, initially built in the 6th and 7th centuries, located on Sioni Street. The current version of the church is based on a 13th-century restoration and some changes from the 17th and 19th centuries. The cathedral was named after the name of Mount Zion at Jerusalem.

- *Metekhi Church* – located on the left bank of the River Mtkvari in the historic neighborhood Metekhi, it was

constructed by the Georgian king Saint Demetrius II
from 1278 to 1284. The King Rostom later fortified
the area with a strong citadel garrisoned by 3000
soldiers.

- *The Lurji Monastery* – also referred to as the *Blue
  Monastery* (*"lurji"* meaning *"blue"*). Constructed in the
  12th century in the name of Saint Andrew, the church
  is located in the Vere neighborhood (Vere Park). The
  name is derived from its roof tile made of glazed blue
  tiles.

- *The Catholic Cathedral of Virgin Mary Ascension* –
  Roman Catholic cathedral located in Tbilisi on G.
  Abesadze street. Even though it dates back to 13th
  century, the present version of the church was
  constructed from 1805 to 1808 by the monk Philipo
  Foranian.

- *The Great Synagogue* – located at 45-47 Leselidze
  Street. Georgian Synagogue was built in eclectic style
  during 1895-1903 by Georgian Jews from Akhaltsikhe
  who migrated to Tbilisi. For that reason, the
  synagogue is also called *"Synagogue of the People of
  Akhaltsikhe."*

- *Sunnite Mosque* – constructed during 1723-1735, the
  mosque is located at the end of the Botanical Garden.
  Even though there had been several other mosques

built in Tbilisi, this is the only functioning one at present. The mosque was built during the Osman reign but was destroyed in the middle of the 17th by the command of Nadir-Shah. The current version of the mosque was restored during 1846-1851.

Neighborhoods Worth Visiting

There are various streets and avenues in Tbilisi especially popular for tourists. Therefore, these areas are also appreciated by local people. Even though it is almost impossible to list all the places that you might enjoy, this section provides information about several neighborhoods that are worth visiting in Tbilisi.

- *Rustaveli Avenue* – central avenue in Tbilisi named after the medieval Georgian poet, Shota Rustaveli. Extending for about 1.5km in length, the avenue comprises various governmental, public, cultural, and business buildings. Several examples include Biltmore Hotel Tbilisi, former Parliament of Georgia, Kashveti Church, Georgian National Opera Theater, Rustaveli State Academic Theatre, and Georgian Academy of Sciences. Moreover, there are diverse restaurants and shopping spots. The easiest way to get to the avenue is by subway. Choose either Metro Station Rustaveli or Metro Station Freedom Square since Rustaveli Avenue stretches between these two stations.

- *Freedom Square* – located at the eastern end of Rustaveli Avenue. The major landmark of the area is the Freedom Monument of Saint George in the center of the square. You can get to the Freedom Square employing the subway (choose Metro Station

Freedom Square). You can walk through the streets of Old Tbilisi directly from the Freedom Square.

- *Aghmashenebeli Avenue* – one of the longest and most eye-catching streets in Tbilisi. You can find breathtaking historic buildings characterized by various architectural ornaments. Since there is a diverse variety of ethnic restaurants in other countries, you might even feel that you are not in Georgia. Although, the avenue is so beautiful that it is worth visiting. To get there, you can take a subway and choose Metro Station Marjanishvili.

- *Old Tbilisi* – a former distinct administrative entity that incorporates several historic neighborhoods in the following districts: Mtatsminda-Krtsanisi, Isani-Samgori, and Didube-Chughureti. The district situated on both sides of the River Mtkvari comprises significant urban and architectural value along with the threat to its survival. The area is predominantly depicted by Mount Mtatsminda, Narikala Fortress, and the Kartlis Deda Monument. Even though the district was partially renovated, the atmosphere is still linked with the old national culture. Some people also compare the place to the Disney film set. One of the important streets is Shardeni which is occupied with plenty of restaurants, lounge bars, and night clubs. The district also includes Sololaki area, which is a great place to wander around and take pictures. The most convenient way to get to the area is to take a subway and choose Metro Station Avlabari or Metro Station Freedom Square.

Monuments

- *Historical Memorial of Georgia* – also referred to as *the Chronicle of Georgia.* Located on a hill near Tbilisi Sea (Tbilisi Reservoir), the memorial was created by painter, sculptor, and architect Zurab Tsereteli to celebrate 3000 years of Georgian sovereignty and 2000 years of Christianity in Georgia.

- *Monument to Characters of Movie "Mimino"* – located near the Metro Station Avlabari, the monument represents main characters of Georgian movie *"Mimino."* Mimino is a 1977 comedy film which depicts the relationships between Georgians, Armenians, and Russians.

- *Monument of King Vakhtang Gorgasali* – the memorial is set on a cliff on the banks of the River Mtkvari in front of the Metekhi Church.

- *Kartlis Deda* - also referred to as Mother of Kartli (or Georgia). The monument constructed by Georgian sculptor Elguja Amashukeli in 1958 is located on the top of Sololaki hill. The 12-meter aluminum figure of a woman in a national dress is a symbol of a Georgian national character. She holds a bowl of wine in her left hand (for allies) and a sword in her left hand (enemies).

- *Freedom Monument* – commonly referred to as Saint George Statue. It is a 35-meter memorial made of granite and gold located in the center of the Freedom Square. The actual statue, which is 5.6 meters tall, is made of bronze and covered with gold. The monument is a gift to the city from Georgian sculptor Zurab Tsereteli.

- *Shota Rustaveli Statue* – statue located near the Metro Station Rustaveli on Rustaveli Avenue. Shota Rustaveli was a medieval Georgian poet who is considered one of the most significant contributors to Georgian literature. Shota Rustaveli is the author of Georgian national epic poem called *"The Knight in the Panther's Skin"* (*"Vepkhistkaosani"*).

- *Monument Fountain of Falcon and Pheasant* – the monument is a symbol of the legend of founding Tbilisi by King Vakhtang Gorgasali. The location of the memorial is 2 Abano Street.

- *Ilia Chavchavadze and Akaki Tsereteli Statue* – monument constructed in 1957 and located on Rustaveli Avenue, in front of the First Classical Gymnasium. Ilia and Akaki were prominent Georgian writers who tremendously contributed to the development of Georgian literature.

- *Monument of Georgian Soldiers in Russo-Georgian War* – the monument built to honor the memory of Georgian heroes killed during the *August War* in 2008. The 51 meters high statue is in the center of the Heroes Square, near the Tbilisi Zoo.

- *Memorial of Georgian Soldiers* – the monument was built to honor the memory of Georgian heroes killed during the war between Georgians and Soviet army in Abkhazia. Every morning, two soldiers arrive at the memorial near the Heroes Square and stand next to the monument the whole day as a sign of respect.

- *Vladimir Mayakovski Monument* – constructed in 1978 by a sculptor Guram Kordzakhia and an architect Givi Japaridze. The statue is located in Dighomi to honor Russian poet born in Georgia.

- *World War II Memorial* – soviet monument constructed during 1980-1985. It is located in Vake Park.

Nature and Parks

- *The National Botanical Garden of Georgia* – formerly known as *Tbilisi Botanical Garden*. It is located on the southern foothills of the Sololaki Range. The garden was first described in 1671, meaning that the history spans more than 3 centuries. Botanical Garden occupies 161 hectares and comprises over 4500 taxonomic groups.

- *Vake Park* – opened in 1949 it is located in the Vake district at the western end of Chavchavadze Avenue. It is identified as the largest park in Tbilisi with the area of 200 hectares. The park is used for a wide variety of events and gatherings.

- *Rike Park* – situated on the left bank of the River Mtkvari it is identified as the youngest recreational areas in Tbilisi. The park comprises various facilities such as singing and dancing fountains, Narikala Fortress, artificial climbing wall, mega-chess board, children's maze, and footpaths. Rike Park also provides an opportunity of a cable car which takes the visitor up to Narikala. You can walk through the old streets to get to Rike Park or take an Aerial Tramway and enjoy the view of the Old Tbilisi neighborhood.

- *9th of April and Giorgi Leonidze parks* - previously referred to as Alexander's park. Located on the opposite side of the parliament building on the Rustaveli Avenue behind the National Gallery. The upper area of the park is known as 9th of April park which was named after the 1989 events which resulted in 20 deaths and even more injuries due to the anti-Soviet demonstration. On the other hand, the lower part of the park is referred to as Giorgi Leonidze park named in honor of Georgian poet and prose writer.

- *Dedaena Park* – one of the essential parks in Tbilisi since there are different festivals and events held throughout the year. This is a great place to get relaxed or hang out with friends while enjoying the fresh air. The park is located near the embankment and the Public Service Hall (House of Justice)

- *Mziuri Park* – the park was significantly damaged during the flooding on 13th of June in 2015, which resulted in 19 deaths. The park is located right in the heart of the city the entrance of which is from Chavchavadze Avenue. Moreover, it is a very popular destination for tourists

- *Mount Mtatsminda* – located on the right bank of the River Mtkvari (Kura), it is one of the most frequently visited place by tourists. The area comprises various entertaining facilities including Mtatsminda Park. To get to the park, you can either take a bus (N90 or N124) from Rustaveli Avenue (near to the Metro Station Rustaveli) or by funicular.

- *Lisi Lake* – located near to the neighborhood Vedzisi and Nutsubidze Plato. It is an excellent place for picnics with friends or family, running, cycling, walking your dog, or spending time with your children. The temperature is usually warm during late spring, summer, and early autumn months but be aware that the temperature is quite low during late autumn, winter, and early spring period and strong winds are also characteristic.

- *Turtle Lake* – also referred to as Kus Tba ("Ku" meaning "Turtle," "Tba" meaning "Lake"). Located in the region of Vake-Saburtalo on the left cliff of Mount Mtatsminda, the height of the place is almost 700m. You can take an Aerial Tramway from Chavchavadze Avenue directly to the Turtle Lake. Moreover, you can get to the lake quickly from Vake Park. If you want to get to the lake by car, it is possible as well by simply following the road from Chavchavadze Avenue which leads to the lake.

- *Tbilisi Sea* – also referred to as Tbilisi Reservoir. It is an artificial lake with a length of 8.75km and width of 2.85km. Currently, there are not many sights or entertaining facilities there, but there are still some, including the Tbilisi Sea Club equipped with large pools. Therefore, it is planned to create a recreational park with various sports facilities.

Museums

MUSEUM: ADDRESS

Phone Number
Website

Georgian National Museum

3 Rustaveli Ave.
+995-32-2-99-80-22
http://www.museum.ge/

Open Air Museum of Ethnography
15 M. Berdzenishvili Str. (Turtle Lake Road)
+995-32-2-72-90-45
http://www.museum.ge/

The National Gallery
1 Rustaveli Ave
+995-32-2-15-73-00
http://www.museum.ge/

Museum of Illusions
10 Betlemi Str
+995-596-04-74-74
https://www.museumofillusions.ge/

State Museum of Theatre, Music, and Cinema
6 Kargareteli Str.
+995-32-2-95-35-63
http://www.artpalace.ge/eng/

Georgian Museum of Fine Arts
7 Rustaveli Ave.
+995-544-44-45-44
http://finearts.ge/

Museum of Modern Art – Zurab Tsereteli
27 Rustaveli Ave.

+995-32-2-14-84-11
http://www.tbilisimoma.ge/

State Museum of Georgian Folk Music and Musical Instruments
6 Samghebro Str.
+995-32-2-45-77-21
N/A
Tbilisi History Museum
8 Sioni Str.
+995-32-2-98-22-81
http://www.museum.ge/

Shalva Amiranashvili Museum of Fine Arts
1 L. Gudiashvili Str.
+995-32-2-99-99-09
N/A
Tbilisi Antique Archeological Museum
Abano Str. Lane, Bling Alleys 1
N/A
N/A

1. **Entertainment**

Shopping Centers
Tbilisi Mall
D. Aghmashenebeli Alley, 16th Km
+995 32 250 55 56
www.tbilisimall.com/en
East Point
2 A. Tvalchrelidze Str.
+995 32 293 00 07
www.eastpoint.ge
Galleria Tbilisi
2/4 Rustaveli Ave.
+995 32 250 00 40

www.galleria.ge
Lilo Mall
112 Kakheti Highway
+995 32 240 70 06
www.lilomall.ge
City Mall Saburtalo
1 Kavtaradze Str.
+995 32 298 75 89
www.thecitymall.ge
City Mall Gldani
1 Khizabavri Str.
+995 32 298 75 89
www.thecitymall.ge
Karvasla
7 Cotne Dadiani Str.
+995 32 266 88 31
www.karvaslamall.ge
Tbilisi Central
Station Square 2
+995 32 235 03 10
https://www.facebook.com/TbilisiCentral/
Merani Mall
42 Rustaveli Ave.
+995 32 299 81 68
www.merani.ge
Kidobani Trading Center
7 G. Tsabadze Str.
+995 571 66 66 13
N/A

Along with the modern shopping centers provided in the table above, there are various local markets in different districts of Tbilisi. Such markets are either referred to as *"Flea Market"* or *"Bazaar."* The list of major local markets along with corre-sponding addresses, is provided below:

- Dry Bridge Flea Market starting from Zaarbriuken Square (near to 2/8 Uznadze Str.)
- Navtlughi Bazaar 91 Queen Ketevan Ave.
- Dezerter Bazaar 5 Abastumani Str.

Cinema and Theatre

Cavea Cinema
Galleria Tbilisi;
Tbilisi Mall;
East Point
+995-32-2-55-50-00
+995-32-2-00-70-07
https://www.cavea.ge/
Amirani Cinema
36/1 Merab Kostava Str.
+995-32-2-55-50-00
N/A
Movement Theatre
182 Aghmashenebeli Ave.
+995-599-56-87-57
https://movementtheatre.ge/
Shota Rustaveli State Dramatic Theatre
17 Rustaveli Ave.
+995-32-2-72-68-68

http://rustavelitheatre.ge/
Zakaria Paliashvili Opera and Ballet Theatre
25 Rustaveli Ave.
+995-32-2-14-32-03
http://www.opera.ge/
Kote Marjanishvili State Academic Theatre
8 Marjanishvili Ave.
+995-32-2-95-40-01

. . .

http://www.marjanishvili.com/
    Music and Drama State Theatre
    182 Aghmashenebeli Ave.
    +995-32-2-34-80-90
    +995-32-2-34-80-90
    http://www.musictheatre.ge/
    Griboedov Russian State Drama Theatre
    2 Rustaveli Ave.
    +995-32-2-93-58-11
    +995-32-2-93-18-40
    http://griboedovtheatre.ge/

Finger Theatre
    8 Marjanishvili Str.
    +995-32-2-95-35-82
    N/A
    Tbilisi State Marionette Theatre
    26 Shavteli Str.
    +995-32-2-98-65-90
    N/A

Amusement Parks and Areas

Mtatsminda Park
    9 Kakutsa Cholokashvili Str
    +995-591-49-23-23
    https://park.ge/ka/

Mushtaidi Park
    182 Aghmashenebeli Ave.
    +995-32-2-34-17-82
    N/A
    Tbilisi Zoo

64 Meraba Kostava Str.
+995-32-2-21-30-60
http://www.zoo.ge/

Contact Zoo – Zootopia
Aghmashenebeli Alley, 16th Km (Tbilisi Mall)
+995-597-74-74-96
https://www.facebook.com/zoozootopia/

Focus Mokus
2 Tvalchrelidze Str. (East Point)
+995-555-07-55-55
http://focusmokus.ge/ka/home
Europark
3 V. Ninua Str.
+995-32-2-69-71-00
https://www.facebook.com/europarki
Gino Paradise
9 Beshenova /8Liptova Str.
+995-32-2-15-85-85
https://ginoparadise.ge/
Astra Park
8 K. Chachava Str.
+995-32-2-37-37-37
https://www.facebook.com/AstraPark/

Casinos and Gambling
Shangri La Casino
River Mtkvari Right Embankment
+995-32-2-20-07-01
https://shangrila.ge/

Jewel Casino

29 Rustaveli Ave. (The Biltmore Hotel)
+995-32-2-60-00-00
http://www.thejewelcasino.com/

Casino Iveria
1 Rose Revolution Square
+995-32-2-40-22-45
http://casinoiveria.com/

Ambassadori Casino
17 Ioane Shavteli Str.
+995-32-2-11-21-21
http://ambassadori.casino/

Casino Adjara
26 May Square
+995-32-2-33-55-19
https://casinoadjara.com/

- **Accommodation**

Popular Hotels in Tbilisi

Mercure Tbilisi Old Town
9 Vakhtang Gorgasali Str.
+995-32-2-00-60-60
N/A
From 470 GEL
Holiday Inn
26 May Square
+995-32-2-30-00-99
https://www.ihg.com/holidayinn/hotels/us/en/tbilisi/

From 450 GEL

Radisson Blu Iveria
1 Rose Revolution Square
+995-32-2-40-22-00
https://www.radissonhotels.com/en-us/hotels/radisson-blu-tbilisi
From 430 GEL
Cortyard Marriott
13 Rustaveli Ave.;
Freedom Square 4.

+995-32-2-77-92-00
+995-32-2-77-92-10
+995-32-2-77-91-00
https://www.marriott.com/

From 360 GEL
Armazi Palace
8 Armazi Str.
+995-32-2-14-40-62
http://www.armazipalace.ge/
From 310 GEL
The Biltmore Hotel
29 Rustaveli Ave.
+995-32-2-72-72-72
N/A
From 300 GEL
No12 Boutique
14 Vakhtang Beridze Str.
+995-32-2-55-22-12
N/A
From 290 GEL
Terrace Boutique

7 Polikarpe Kakabadze Str.
+995-32-2-99-90-01
N/A
From 290 GEL
Margo Palace
12 Elbakidze Str.
+995-32-2-43-60-40
http://margopalace.com/

From 290 GEL
Preference Hualing
Tbilisi Sea
+995-32-2-50-50-25
http://www.hotelspreference.ge/

From 270 GEL
Tbilisi Inn
20 Metekhi Str.
+995-32-2-77-00-50
http://tbilisiinn.com/ge

From 250 GEL
Orion
5 Napareuli Str.
+995-32-2-55-25-55
http://www.hotelorion.ge/Tbilisi/

From 250 GEL
Sheraton Metekhi Palace
20 Kuchishvili Str.
+995-32-2-77-20-20
N/A
From 250 GEL

Vere Palace
22-24 Kuchishvili Str.
+995-32-2-25-33-40
http://www.verepalace.com.ge/

From 250 GEL
Citadel Narikala
20 Orpiri Str.
+995-32-2-90-41-41
http://www.hotel-citadel.ge/

From 250 GEL
Coral Boutique
113b Dimitri Uznadze Str.
+995-32-2-43-01-13
http://coralhotel.ge/

From 190 GEL
Residence Hill Plus
110 T. Tabidze Str.
+995-555-51-43-02
N/A
From 80 GEL
Calista
2 Tsernaki Str.
+995-593-78-00-78
N/A
From 80 GEL
Batoni
1 Mamisashvili Str.
+995-599-77-18-88
N/A
From 80 GEL
Okriba

2 Didube Str.
+995-599-98-20-43
N/A
From 70 GEL
Pyramide
19 Zestafoni Str.
+995-591-44-91-41
N/A
From 60 GEL

AUTONOMOUS REPUBLIC OF ABKHAZIA

New Athos Monastery

- **Geography and Demographics.**

Abkhazia is a de facto sovereign region in the South Caucasus on the eastern coast of the Black Sea and the south of the Greater Caucasus Mountains in northwestern Georgia. With a

population of around 240,000, it covers the area of 8,660km².
The capital city of Abkhazia is Sukhumi.

The population of Abkhazia is mainly comprised of ethnic
Abkhaz (50.8%), Georgians (mainly Megrelians), Hemshin
Armenians, and Russians. Some other ethnic groups include
Belarusians, Greeks, Ukrainians, Ossetians, Tatars, Turks, and
Roma.

Abkhazia and the Russian Federation are divided by the
Caucasus Mountains to the north and northeast. Abkhazia is
bounded by Samegrelo-Zemo Svaneti region to the east and
southeast. It borders the Black Sea on the south and southwest.

Abkhazia comprises a wide variety of geographical areas
including lowlands, mountains, small rivers, and caves.

- **Climate and Seasonality**

The weather in Abkhazia is very mild due to its proximity to the
Black Sea and the shield of the Caucasus Mountains. The coastal
areas of Abkhazia have Subtropical climate with an average
annual temperature around 15°C (in most regions). The average
temperature in winter (in January specifically) remains above
the freezing point. On the other hand, the climate at higher
elevations varies from Maritime Mountainous to Cold and even
Summerless.

Because of its position, mountains of Abkhazia receive high
amounts of precipitation and significant amounts of snow.

Considering the information provided above, the best
seasons to visit Abkhazia are late spring, summer, and early
autumn.

Beach season lasts from mid-Mary till October.

- **History**

The history of Abkhazia is quite comprehensive, and it is almost
impossible to narrate the entire history. Therefore, this travel-

er's guide provides key events and essential periods for Abkhazia.

The history of Abkhazia begins with the coming of the Milesian Greeks to the Coastal Colchis in the 6th-5th centuries BC. The city was named Dioscuri. Along with the rest of Colchis, the area was conquered by Mithridates VI Eupator of Pontus (110-63 BC). Later the territories were taken by the Roman commander Pompey. As a result, modern-day Abkhazia was incorporated into the Roman Empire.

From 542 to 562, Byzantines built Sebastopolis in the region. The land of Byzantines was referred to as Abasgia. During the medieval period, Abasgi became stronger and included various ethnic groups such as Mingrelian- and Svan-speaking South Caucasian tribes. Abkhazia reached its prosperity from 850 to 950 when it dominated the whole western Georgia and has control even on the eastern Georgian provinces.

The fort of Tskhumi on the Abkhazian coastline was turned into the Turkish fortress of Suhum-Kale by the Ottoman navy in the 1507s. In 1555, Georgia and the whole South Caucasus region were divided between Ottoman and Safavid Persians. At the end of the 17th century, Abkhazia became the site of widespread slave trade and piracy. Even though Abkhazians took hold of Suhum-Kale in the mid-18th century, Turks regained the control over the fortress and granted it to the prince of the Shervashidze family.

In 1800, Russia annexed the eastern part of Georgia and took over Mingrelia in 1803. Large part of the population was displaced to Turkey, and in 1877 the population of Abkhazia decreased from 78,000 to 46,000. Since there were lots of uninhabited areas left, Armenians, Georgians, and Russians migrated to Abkhazia.

On February 11th in 1921, Soviet Russia's 11th Red Army invaded Georgia and entered Tbilisi. Almost at the same time, 9th Arm marched on Abkhazia. As a result, Soviet power was established in Sukhumi on March 4th.

At the end of the 1980s, the Soviet Union began to disintegrate, and ethnic tension between the Abkhaz and Georgian people grew. Abkhazians were afraid of losing autonomy in case of Georgia's independence and proposed establishing Abkhazia as a separate Soviet republic. The war in Abkhazia began in August of 1992 (Georgian government forces and a militia comprising ethnic Georgians living in Abkhazia VS Russian-backed separatist forces involving ethnic Abkhazians, Armenians, and Russians also living in Abkhazia). The war lasted for 13 months and is considered as one of the bloodiest in the post-Soviet areas.

After a couple of years, Abkhazia was self-proclaimed as an independent Republic. In 2008, after the Russo-Georgian war, Russia recognized Abkhazia as a country.

As a consequent, relations between Abkhazia and Georgia remain intense. Georgians consider Abkhazia as a part of their country. There are still some issues regarding this aspect; that is why you should always be careful while traveling in this area.

• Religion and Language

Major religions in Abkhazia are identified to be Christianity and Islam. Some minor religions include Judaism, Jehovah's Witnesses, and other new religious movements. Despite the difference in religious beliefs, they all have equal rights before the law.

According to Article 6 of the Constitution of Abkhazia, the official language of the Republic of Abkhazia is Abkhazian (Abkhaz). Along with that, Russian is recognized as a language of State and other agencies. Other languages spoken within Abkhazia are Megrelian, Svan, Armenian, and Greek. Moreover, English is used in tourist centers.

• How to get to Abkhazia

For traveling to Abkhazia, the foreign citizens are required to have a double-entry or multiple Russian Visa since you go by transit through Russia.

You can get to Abkhazia by air from any city throughout the world to the Sochi International Airport (Russian Federation). After that, you should cross the Russian-Abkhaz border by taking/ordering taxi and driving for about 30 minutes.

Here are several Taxi services you can use:

- *Sukhum Taxi*
- Tel: +7 940 716 00 00; +7 840 226 00 00
- E-mail: abhaztaxi@mail.ru
- Website: www.abhaztaxi.ru
- *Garuda-Express*
- Tel: +7 940 990 01 11; +7 940 77 21 11

In case if you are traveling to Abkhazia from Georgia, you first need to get to a border city Zugdidi. After that, you have to get a Taxi to get to the border. There are 4 stages for entering Abkhazia, which are the following:

- 20 minutes to the Georgian border. There is no need for stamping your passport since Georgians do not perceive crossing this border as leaving the country.

- 2-3km across the bridge that goes over Enguri river.

- 30 minutes to Abkhazian border

- Russian checkpoint

*Important Note – if you are traveling from Russia to Abkhazia, you are not allowed to leave through/enter Georgia since Georgia does not recognize the border. On the contrary, if you enter Abkhazia through Georgia, you are generally allowed to enter Russia, but you might be banned from entering Georgia or be required to pay a fine.

- **Money and Currency**

The official currency of the Republic of Abkhazia is the Russian Ruble. You can exchange currency in any bank of Abkhazia. Due to the fact that the use of any plastic card (Eurocard, MasterCard, Visa International, American Express) for payments is currently prohibited throughout Abkhazia, you should cash the money in ATMs.

The limit for the undeclared import of foreign currency is $3,000 per person. If the cash is over $3,000 per person, the currency must be declared to the customs service. In the case of cash import of over $10,000 per person, individuals must receive permission from the Central Bank.

• Mobile Operators and Telephone Communication

There are two mobile operators in Abkhazia:

- *A-Mobile*
- Address: 384900 Gumistinskaiya Str.14; Sukhumi, Novy Raion
- Tel: +7 940 999 99 99
- E-mail: info@aquafon.com
- Website: www.aquafon.com
- *Aquafon*
- Address: 384900 Kodorskoe Shosse Str.665; Sukhumi, Sinop
- Tel: +7 840 229 40 18; +7 840 229 40 19; +7 940 777 77 77
- E-mail: info@a-mobile.biz
- Website: www.a-mobile.biz

For international calls dial: 8-10 + City Code + Phone Number
For calls to Russia dial: 8-107 + City Code + Phone Number

• Highlights of Abkhazia

Abkhazia is a fantastic destination you cannot miss. Considering the political situation, when you travel to Abkhazia, it feels like you go to another country rather than Georgia. Be extremely cautious while traveling to Abkhazia. Always try to be accompanied by a local person you trust.

Most popular tourist sights in Abkhazia are provided below:

- **Gagra** – a town in Abkhazia. The climate in Gagra is subtropical, which makes it a popular health resort. What makes the place unique is its views over the mountainous areas and the bay.

There are lots of exciting places to visit in Gagra, including but not limited to the following:

- *Ruins of the Abaata Fortress* – built in the 4th-5th centuries AD. Fortress is located at the end of the northern end of Primorsky Park in Old Gagra.

- *The Cave of Saint Hypatia* – it is believed that in the cave of Saint Hypatia, there lived a monk and hermit Hypatia. It is not that easy to get to the cave; you have to climb the rock at a distance of 12 meters. The cave is located between the New and Old Gagra. It is not recommended to visit the cave during the evening or night hours.

- **Sukhumi** – the capital city of Abkhazia. The climate in Sukhumi is Humid Subtropical. Since it is cool in Summer, it is close to an oceanic environment. Sukhumi comprises several historical sights including but not limited to the following:

- - *The Besleti Bridge* – a medieval arched stone bridge

built during the reign of Tamar Mepe in the 12th century. Spanning the small mountain River Basla (Besleti, Besletka), it is located 6km away from the city center.

- - *Bagrat's Castle* – ruined medieval castle dated to the late 10th or early 11th century close to the Black Sea coast. The fort was named in honor to the Georgian king Bagrat. It is not clear if the castle was named after Bagrat III or Bagrat IV. The castle stands on a hill on the left bank of the River Besleti.

- - *Kelasuri Wall* – also referred to as Great Abkhazian Wall. It is a wall made of stone located in the eastern part of Sukhumi. The exact date of its construction is not known, but it dates somewhere between antiquity to the 17th century. The wall starts from the mouth of Kelasuri River and terminates near the village of Lekukhona on the right bank side of River Enguri.

- - *Sukhumi Botanical Garden* – founded in the 1840s, is considered as one of the oldest botanical gardens in the Caucasus. The Turks ravaged the garden in 1853-1855 and 1877-1878 due to the Russo-Turkish wars. Afterward, the garden was granted to the civil authorities, as a result of which, in 1894 the restoration of the plantings began. Furthermore, the botanical garden also suffered during the Georgian-Abkhazian war.

- Abandoned buildings dominate in Sukhumi. One of the most impressive ones is the *Abandoned Parliament*. The Georgian authorities occupied it in the past, but after the conflict, it remains without any function. There are a lot more similar buildings throughout Sukhumi, so there is no point in listing them all. You can see everything by yourself by simply walking through the streets of Sukhumi.

- **Akhali (New) Athos** – a town in the Gudauta region of Abkhazia. The city was previously known under various names, including Nikopol, Acheisos, Anakopia, Nikopia, Nikopsis, Absara, Psyrtskha. It is considered as the prettiest coastal town in Abkhazia. With about 1,700 years of history, the place is characterized by the blue-turquoise water and dense green forests near the edge of the water.

- *- New Athos Monastery* – built by Russian monks in 1874. The monastery was closed in 1924 due to the Soviet persecution of religion. As a result, it was used as a storage facility, tourist base, hospital, and museum. It was returned to the Orthodox Church in 1994 after the end of the war. It has been a popular tourist destination due to the scenic setting of the monastery by the sea.

- *- New Athos Cave* – located a few kilometers away from the town, it is a karst cave in the Iverian Mountain. It has served as a New Athos Cave Railway

since 1975. The cave is considered as one of the
largest with the total volume of its void of about
1,000,000m^3.

- • - *Hydroelectric Power Station* – New Athos comprises a
small hydroelectric power station along with an
artificial lake on the Psyrtskha River. Located near to
the old Church of Saint Simon the Canaanite, the
station was built by the monks of the monastery from
1892 to 1903. It had been broken for about 40 years
but was re-opened in 2012.

- • - *New Athos Saint Simon Canaanite Monastery* – dates
from the 9th or 10th century. The church was built in
honor to Saint Simon the Canaanite who preached
Christianity in Abkhazia and Egrisi. The visual
characteristics of the church are influenced by the
Byzantine and Georgian art traditions.

- • **Pitsunda** – also referred to as Bichvinta; It is a resort
in the Gagra district of Abkhazia. The resort is famous
for its sandy and pebble beaches with the purest
seawater.

- • - *Pitsunda Beach* – as it was mentioned above, Pitsunda
is characterized by the pure water and clean beach.
For that reason, Pitsunda Beach is worth visiting.

- *- Sculpture Divers* – a magnificent sculpture enjoyed and photographed by many of the tourists. You need to get to the embankment first to get to the statue itself, which is quite easy and worth it.

- *- The Abkhazian National Dolphinarium* – the only Dolphinarium in Abkhazia opened in 2016. Located on the Central Beach of Pitsunda (5 Gitsba Str.), the Dolphinarium offers open sky shows during summer months as well as allows visitors to swim with dolphins in the pool. To enroll in this dolphin therapy course, you should call the Dolphinarium by dialing "+7 940 990 11 90". It costs approximately 700 Rubles for adults and is free for children to 3 years.

- **<u>Ochamchire</u>** – also referred to as Ochamchira. It is a seaside city on the Black Sea coast of Abkhazia. The climate in Ochamchire is Humid Subtropical with hot summers and mild winters.

- *- Abrskil Cave* – stalactite cave in karstic limestone, located in the southern slopes of the Panavi ridge near the port of Ochamchire. The length of the cave is about 2km, but it goes up to 3km if we include the passages. From 1.5 to 1.7km, it has been made accessible. The cave comprises naturally formed stalactites, stalagmites, and helictites.

Accommodation

Popular Hotels in Abkhazia

Wellness Park Hotel Gagra
    52 Sosnalieva Str. (Former Abazgaa),
    384870 Gagra, Georgia
    +7 940 996 72 76
    www.parkhotelgagra.com
    From 350 GEL

Amran
    5 Pionerskaya Str., 384870 Gagra, Georgia
    +7 867 250 11 34
    www.amtransit-inn.my
    From 350 GEL

Napra
    267 Oktyabrskaya Str., 984964 Tsandrypsh, Georgia
    +7 940 992 22 66
    https://www.facebook.com/1499460130164011/
posts/1542291815880842/
    From 300 GEL

Alex Beach
    1 Zvanba Str., 194361 Gagra, Georgia
    +7 940 960 40 70
    www.hotel-alex-beach.ru
    From 250 GEL

Grand Hotel Gagra
    237 Ardzinba Ave., 384870 Gagra, Georgia
    +7 940 734 65 64
    https://www.alean.ru/abkhaziya/gagra/

gagra_gorod/grand_hotel_gagra_otel/
From 250 GEL

Aquamarine
58 Sosnalieva Str. (Former Abazgaa), 384870 Gagra, Georgia
+7 94 932 85 55
www.aquamarinegagra.com
From 200 GEL

Hotel Medoviy
7a Sosnalieva Str. (Former Abazgaa), 384870 Gagra, Georgia
+7 981 810 49 17
https://www.priceline.com/hotel-deals/h47955504/GE/
Abkhazia/Gagra/Hotel-Medoviy.html
From 180 GEL

Ritsa Hotel
2 Leona Ave., 384900 Sukhumi, Georgia
+7 840 223 32 41
www.ritsa-hotel.com
From 180 GEL

Bereg Evkaliptov
26, 7a Oktyabrskaya Str., 384898 Tsandrypsh, Georgia
+7 940 715 61 56
www.beregvkaliptov.ru
From 150 GEL

- **Important Contacts**

- *Ministry of Foreign Affairs of the Republic of Abkhazia*
- Address: 284900 Lakoba Str.21; Sukhumi

- Tel: +7 840 226 70 69
- E-mail: info@mfaapsny.org
- Website: www.mfaapsny.org
- *State Committee for Resorts and Tourism of the Republic of Abkhazia*
- Address: 384900 Prospect Mira Str.119, Sukhumi
- Tel: +7 840 26 37 90
- E-mail: info@abkhazia.travel
- Website: www.abkhazia.travel
- *Emergency Services*
- Fire Department – "01"
- Police – "02"
- Ambulance – "03"

3

SAMEGRELO – ZEMO SVANETI

Fountain in Zugdidi

• Geography and Demographics

Samegrelo – Zemo Svaneti is a region in the western part of Georgia which includes the following historical provinces:

Samegrelo and Zemo Svaneti. The capital of the area is the main city of Samegrelo, Zugdidi.

Samegrelo also referred to as Samegrelo (by Megrelians) and Mingrelia (by foreigners), is a historic province in the western part of Georgia (previously known as Odishi). Mingrelia is bordered by Abkhazia to the northwest, Svaneti to the north, Imereti to the east, Guria to the south, and the Black Sea to the west.

Zemo Svaneti, also referred to as Upper Svaneti (Svanetia) is a historic province in the northwest part of the country. Zemo Svaneti is situated on the upper Inguri River. The central city of Zemo Svaneti is Mestia. Zemo Svaneti is separated from Kvemo Svaneti (Lower Svanetia) by the Svaneti Range.

The population of the region is 316,200 according to the data retrieved in 2018. 98.9% of the whole community is Georgian, and 0.9% is Russian while the remaining percentage comprises minor ethnic groups, including Ukrainians, Armenians, Abkhazians, and Greeks.

- **Climate and Seasonality**

Samegrelo-Zemo Svaneti is one of the warmest regions of Georgia during summer. Average daily temperature is identified to be 22°C.

Since the Black Sea borders the region, the climate in the area is subtropical with frequent rains.

For that reason, the best time to visit Samegrelo-Zemo Svaneti is the late spring or early autumn. But in case if you enjoy winter sports and are looking for new places and challenges, the region will attract your attention through new ski resorts (Hatsvali, Tetnuldi).

- **Religion and Language**

The primary religion of the region is Orthodox Christianity, with about 83% of the whole population identified as Orthodox Christians. Approximately 10% of inhabitants identify themselves as Muslims. Several groups of people of Armenian Christians and Roman Catholics also exist.

The entire population speaks Georgian language while Mingrelians also speak Mingrelian (Kartvelian language) and Svans speak Svan (Kartvelian language).

- **How to get to Samegrelo – Zemo Svaneti**

There are several options to get to the capital of the Samegrelo-Zemo Svaneti region, Zugdidi, which is located 335km away from Tbilisi.

- Via train from Tbilisi:
- Ticket costs about $10
- Departs from railway station located at Station Square (Tbilisi Central Building).
- Official schedules - https://ticket.railway.ge/

- Via minibus (marshrutka) from Tbilisi:
- Ticket costs about $10
- Departs from Tbilisi bus terminal

- Via train from Kutaisi:
- Ticket costs about $10
- Departs from the railway station of Kutaisi
- Official schedules - https://ticket.railway.ge/

- Via minibus from Batumi:

- Ticket costs about $10
- Departures several times a day from Batumi station.

It is also quite easy to get to Mestia. Several options are listed below:

- Via minibus from Zugdidi Railway Station to Mestia
- Ticket costs about $6

- Via minibus from Tbilisi Railway Station to Mestia
- Ticket costs about $10

- Via small plane from Natakhtari Airport to Mestia
- Ticket costs about $25

- **Highlights of Samegrelo – Zemo Svaneti**

- <u>Zugdidi</u> – a city situated in the northwest part of the western Georgian historical province of Samegrelo (also referred to as Mingrelia). Located 318km away from Tbilisi, it is the regional center of Samegrelo-Zemo Svaneti.

- *- Dadiani Palace* – also referred to as Dadiani Palaces Historical and Architectural Museum. It is a national museum established in 1840. The museum contains different goldsmith work samples from 1st century BC to 19th century AD, including but not limited to icons, religious objects, elegant art samples, archeological materials from Greek and Georgian antique culture, relics of Samegrelo princes, Dadiani family, royal families of France, Russia, and Spain. Be aware that the museum works every day except for Monday and the ticket price is just 2GEL ($0.7) for adults and 1GEL ($0.35) for students. Furthermore, children less than 6 years or homeless children are free of charge, along with 1st and 2nd category disabled people, soldiers, and refugees.

- *Zugdidi Botanical Garden* – established by the Prince of Mingrelia David Dadiani and Queen Ekaterine in the 19th century, it is located near the residential palaces. The garden which covers 26 hectares is administered by the Georgian Academy of Sciences and is a part of Tbilisi Central Botanical Garden. The botanical garden incorporates about 80 genera of exotic plants from the Americas, the Mediterranean, Southeast Asia, India, and Japan.

- Natipuru Hut Okhoje Lake Tobavarchkhili Lake Khobistskali Valley Khaishura Valley
- This is the frequent hiking track starting which lasts for 6-7 days. The track starts from Natipuru Hut which is the area beneath the Natipuru mountain. The area opens the panorama of Egrisi mountains. The next destination which is the Okhoje Lake, is situated 10.2km away from Natipuru Hut. If the weather is good, one can even see Elbrus from the beautiful alpine lake. Tobavarchkhili Lake is 6km away from Okhoje Lake, and this is the next destination. It is sometimes considered as the most beautiful lake in Georgia. The next destination is Khobistskali Valley

(7.3km from the last lake). The final destination of the track is Khaishura Valley which is 14.3km far from Khobistskali Valley. The valley opens breathtaking panorama of the Greater Caucasus.

- - *Tsaishi Cathedral* – also referred to as the Church of the Assumption of the Holy Mother of God. It is one of the oldest cathedrals in Georgia dating back to 6th-7th centuries.

- **Martvili** – a small town located in Samegrelo region near the River Abashistskali (280km away from Tbilisi). The area is typically known for its mesmerizing canyons and nature.

- - *Martvili Monastery* – also referred to as Chkondidi (meaning "big oak" in Mingrelian). Situated on a small hill, the monastery is seen from the entrance of the town. According to legend, the present-day monastery was built on a place on which a large oak tree stood. The oak tree was a symbol of prosperity and fertility for the pagan people. When Christianity came to Georgia, the tree which people worshiped was cut down, and a church was constructed. Since Christianity in the region was preached by Saint Andrew, the church was named right after him. One can reach the monastery by car, on foot, or using funicular that goes from Martvili.

- - Martvili Canyon – located in Samegrelo, it is considered as a natural wonder. It is a top-rated tourist site which offers the scenery, waterfalls, 300-meter boat trips, diving, and even civil marriage ceremony. Moreover, tourists can enjoy Dadianis' Path, mountain river gorge, natural limestone bridges, water mill from the 19th century, sea urchins, and fossil shells of nautiluses. Entrance fee for foreign citizens is 15GEL ($5), for a boat trip you need an extra 13GEL ($4.4) per person, diving costs 50GEL ($17), and the fee for the marriage ceremony is 100GEL ($34).

- **Poti** – located 312km away from Tbilisi on the eastern Black Sea coast, it is a port city built near the site of the ancient Greek colony of Phasis. It houses the main naval base and the headquarters of Georgian Navy.

- - *Paliastomi Lake* – small lake (surface area of 17.3km^2) near the city of Poti which is connected to the Black Sea by a narrow channel. You can rent a boat and go on a boat trip following one of the several routes on the lake. You can observe the migration of groups of birds, some of which even include rare species. Pontoon boat for 16 people costs approximately 180GEL ($61).

- - *Kolkheti National Park* – located in Samegrelo-Zemo Svaneti and Guria. It comprises a large area of natural wetlands that are especially popular for visitors enjoying birdwatching. The natural park area is considered to be the homeland of the legendary Kolkhi Pheasant. The region comprises 194 distinct bird species, including 21 species of migrating birds.

- - *Poti Lighthouse* – considered as one of the oldest navigation systems on the Black Sea coast. The lighthouse made of cast iron was constructed in England in 1864. The lighthouse not only decorates the city and opens spectacular views of the area but also remains active.

- - *Nino Nikoladze Tower* – also referred to as Old Clock Tower in Poti or simply Poti Tower. It is the oldest building in Poti which was a former Turkish fortress in the late 16th century. The mosque was destroyed at the end of Turkish domination and retouched by Niko Nikoladze by adding 2 floors and a clock manufactured in France in the 19th century.

- - *Poti Cathedral* – also referred to as Poti Soboro Cathedral located in downtown Poti. It is a Georgian Orthodox church constructed from 1907 to 1907 as an imitation of Hagia Sophia in Istanbul. The church depicts one of the earliest uses of reinforced concrete applied to a church (for the foundations and the entire construction).

- - *Poti Museum of Colchian Culture* – located in the historic building, the museum operates since 1933.

The museum incorporates various archeological and ethnographic artifacts of the historical region of Kolkheti from 3000 BC till the 16th century AD. Moreover, objects of antique ceramics, as well as golden coins of famous rulers (Alexander the Great, the Byzantine Emperor Justinian, the Russian Empress Elizaveta), are also represented.

- **Anaklia** – seaside resort at the area where the Enguri River flows into the Black Sea. It is situated near the administrative border with Abkhazia. The earliest settlements on the territory of modern-day Anaklia date back to the mid-Bronze Age and is characteristic to the Colchian culture. The area comprises several most fabulous hotels. Since 2015, the resort has been hosting the largest electronic music festival in Georgia, GEM Fest.

- *- Anaklia-Ganmukhuri Pedestrian Bridge* – considered as the longest cable-stayed timber bridge in Europe and the world. It serves as a linkage across the Enguri River to the town of Anaklia. It is a vital bridge for tourist destinations of Anaklia. Tourists have especially enjoyed the design and the system of the lighting of the bridge. The bridge is particularly stunning at nighttime.

- *- Anaklia Aqua Park* – situated right next to the Anaklia-Ganmukhuri Pedestrian Bridge mentioned above. Aquapark comprises several extreme slides for individuals enjoying an adrenaline rush. The territory

is well-equipped with facilities that one might need.
Moreover, there is a small café within the aqua park
for drinks and snacks. This place is a very good place
for adults as well as kids. You can spend a full day at
the park for only about 15GEL ($5).

- **Mestia** – regional center of Zemo Svaneti. Located
  456km away from Tbilisi, it is 1,500 meters above the
  sea level. Mestia comprises glaciers near mount
  Ushba, pristine alpine meadows, ski resorts, and
  plenty of wall paintings, frescoes, and icons from the
  Middle Ages in the churches.

- *- Ski resort Hatsvali* – located in Svaneti, about 8km
  away from Mestia. Hatsvali is connected to Mestia by
  the automobile road as well as the six-chair ski lift. Be
  aware that the ski lift is closed during the summer
  months (sometimes in October and November too) so
  in case if you want to visit Hatsvali in summer, you
  will need a car for transportation. You can either take
  a taxi or travel by your own car. Since the road is
  paved, there will not be any barrier for any type of car.
  As you reach the Mount Zuruldi, you will enjoy the
  unique views of the snowy slopes of Tetnuldi and the
  Caucasus Mountains range.

- *- Ski resort Tetnuldi* – located in Svaneti, near Mestia. It
  is the second biggest winter resort in Georgia (after
  Gudauri). 3 POMA lifts can be used for transportation
  from 1600m to 3165m altitude. There are trails with
  different difficulty levels, the longest of which is

9.5km long. Since Tetnuldi is so close to Mestia, you can simply take a taxi or a bus for transportation.

- *- Chaladi Glacier* – located on the southern slopes of the Caucasus Mountains. It is the only glacier in the region that extends into a forest zone. The track is relatively moderate which takes up to 6 hours to walk to the glacier and back to Mestia.

- *- Koruldi Lakes* – located in the surrounding area of Mestia. The lakes lie at the base of Mount Ushba. Situated at 2,200m above the sea level, the area offers gorgeous views of the vicinity of Mestia. It takes approximately 4 hours of hiking, and the track is quite well marked.

- *- Ushguli* – located 2-3 hours drive away from Mestia, it is the highest settlement in Europe (at the elevation of 2,200m above the sea level). The small village lying at the base of Mount Shkhara and offer breathtaking views of green slopes, various defense towers, and snowy mountain peaks.

- *- Svaneti Historical and Ethnography Museum* – founded in 1936, the museum comprises a diverse variety of historical artifacts from the Svaneti region (unique icons, engravings, collection of manuscripts, iron/silver/copper ornaments, pottery, jewelry, medieval weapons, and textile items). All the ethnographic items housed in the museum represent the ancient lifestyle in Svaneti.

- - *Museum of Michael Khergiani* – the museum comprises personal items of Michael Khergiani, famous alpinist. The ground floor houses climbing equipment, clothing, photos, awards, and gifts which include musical records by Vladimir Vysotsky dedicated to Khergiani.

- - *Transfiguration Cathedral in Laghami* – located in the oldest part of Mestia. It is a two-story basilica the first floor of which is named in honor of Great Martyr Barbara and dates back to the 9th century. Moreover, the second floor was constructed from the 13th to 14th centuries and depicts various frescoes. Northern and eastern walls of basilica represent the "Banishment of Adam and Eve from the Garden of Eden" and the "Hunting of Saint Eustaphios" respectively. More importantly, the cathedral comprises a 13th-century icon of Christ engraved in gold and silver.

- - *Ipari-Nakipari Church of Saint George* – 11th-century church located in Kala, Mestia. The church houses an engraved icon of Saint George which was crafted by an 11th-century goldsmith. Moreover, the eastern façade of the church depicts various animals.

- **Ushguli** – community which incorporates 4 villages

(Zhibiani, Chvibiani/Chubiani, Chazhashi/Chajashi, Murkmeli) located at the head of the Enguri gorge. The area is considered as the UNESCO World Heritage Site due to its highest inhabited settlements in Europe. Located near the foot of Shkhara mountain, it is not as accessible as Mestia or other more developed regions of Zemo Svaneti. The area is characterized by defensive towers typical to Svaneti region.

- *- Shkhara Glacier* – a popular destination for individuals enjoying hiking. The hike route starts in Ushguli and lasts for about 5 hours. Since you just walk at the bottom of the valley, the difficulty of the track is considered to be easy. Even though you have to walk on a dirt track, the views of Shkhara mountain are really nice, so it is worth it.

- *- Ushguli Ethnographic Museum* – located in the 12th-century building (one of the oldest buildings in Ushguli), it is a tiny museum that comprises items of Svanetian people from middle ages to late 19th century. Tourists consider the place as one of the most exciting destinations in Ushguli.

- *- Lamaria Church* – also referred to as the Church of the Assumption of the Holy Mother of God. Standing on a lonely hill, the church from the 9th century is embedded in beautiful nature with a breathtaking view of Mount Shkhara. The fact that the church is usually lighted by candles (due to the

lack of sunlight) makes the church even more
mysterious and unique.

- **Accommodation**

Popular Hotels in Anaklia
Anaklia
Anaklia, Zugdidi
+995 32 260 99 90
www.hotelanaklia.com
From 130 GEL
Palm Beach Hotel
237 Rustaveli Str.
+995 596 00 77 00
www.pbanaklia.ge
From 100 GEL
Twins
235 Rustaveli Str.
+995 32 260 99 90
https://bit.ly/2nEn2Ss
From 60 GEL
Cruise
268 Rustaveli Str.
+995 568 79 79 99
https://bit.ly/2mKJd9D
From 55 GEL

Popular Hotels in Martvili
Resort Martvili
8 Tavisupleba Str. (3rd floor)
+995 598 40 45 77
https://www.facebook.com/pages/category/Beach-Resort/
Resort-Martvili-228142581385296/
From 180 GEL

Martvili Palace
8 Mshvidoba Str.
+995 593 80 07 00
https://www.facebook.com/martvilipalace/
From 140 GEL
Hotel Alley
1 Zemo Nagvazao Str.
+995 598 69 94 14
N/A
From 90 GEL
Canyon Hotel
12 Chavchavadze Str.
+995 591 31 31 33
https://bit.ly/2m1jZmZ
From 60 GEL

Popular Hotels in Mestia

Hotel Svaneti
5 Queen Tamar Str.
+995 599 57 28 50
https://bit.ly/2m1kbTg
From 150 GEL
Hotel Banguriani
Margiani Str., 3200 Mestia
+995 596 11 26 26
http://www.banguriani.com/
From 140 GEL
Lileo Hotel
9 Z. Phaliani Str.
+995 599 55 03 66
https://bit.ly/2oimLoL
From 120 GEL
Hotel Old Seti
11 Anjaparidze Str.
+995 551 31 91 94
oldseti@yahoo.com

From 100 GEL

Popular Hotels in Zugdidi

BookHouse
32 Tsaishvili Str.
+995 558 88 81 11
https://bit.ly/2m76Nx6
From 250 GEL
Rivers Hotel
55 Bako Str.
+995 593 03 60 00
www.rivers.ge
From 250 GEL
Iberia Palace Hotel
6 Kikalishvili Str.
+995 592 75 09 90
https://bit.ly/2odMf6A
From 230 GEL
Hotel Grand
35 Gamsakhurdia Str.
+995 597 77 77 01
https://bit.ly/2ojN2Dd
From 150 GEL

Popular Hotels in Poti

Prime Poti
53 Akaki Str.
N/A
https://bit.ly/2odCXrb
From 220 GEL

- **Important Contacts**

- *Mestia Tourist Information Center*
- Address: Seti Square 7, Mestia
- Tel: +995 551 08 08 94
- E-mail: ticmestia@gmail.com
- Website: https://georgia.travel; www.gnta.ge
- *Zugdidi Tourist Information Center*
- Address: Rustaveli Str. 87, Zugdidi
- Tel: +995 591 44 53 45; +995 598 46 92 01
- E-mail: ticzugdidi@gmail.com
- Website: https://georgia.travel; www.gnta.ge
- *Martvili Tourist Information Center*
- Address: Tavisufleba Str. 7, Martvili
- Tel: +995 577 78 77 73; +995 568 16 08 08
- E-mail: ticmartvili@gmail.com
- Website: https://georgia.travel; www.gnta.ge
- *Chkhorotsku Tourist Information Center*
- Address: Davit Aghmashenebeli Str. 2, Chkhorotsku
- Tel: +995 417 22 15 66
- E-mail: ticchkhorotsku@gmail.com
- Website: https://georgia.travel; www.gnta.ge

4

RACHA-LECHKHUMI – KVEMO SVANETI

- **Geography and Demographics**

Racha-Lechkhumi – Kvemo Svaneti is a region in the northwest of Georgia. The area comprises historical provinces of Racha, Lechkhumi, ad Kvemo Svaneti (Lower Svanetia). The region overlaps with a section of northwest South Ossetia, but Georgia has no jurisdiction and control over the de facto Republic of South Ossetia. The area consists of 4 administrative units: municipalities of Ambrolauri, Lentekhi, Oni, and Tsageri. The capital of the region is Ambrolauri.

Covering an area of 4,954km^2, it has a population of about 32,000. Almost the entire community is ethnic Georgian (99%) while the remaining 1% is composed of Russians, Azerbaijanians, Ossetians, and Abkhazians.

- **Climate and Seasonality**

The weather in the region is quite warm during summer days but cold at night (even in summer). There are of course some exceptions, but if you travel in the region you should pack warm clothes for chilly evenings and nights. Since the precipitation level is high during winter months, it is recommended to visit the region in late spring, summer, or early autumn to fully enjoy the natural beauty.

- **Religion and Language**

The majority of the population identifies themselves as Orthodox Christians while there are still some minor religious groups within the region. The language spoken by the entire community is Georgian. Moreover, the Svan language is also spoken by the elders in Kvemo Svaneti.

- **How to get to Racha-Lechkhumi – Kvemo Svaneti**

You can get to various parts of the region from the minibus station (Okriba) near Metro Station Didube. The area is connected with other regions mostly by roads, so the most convenient way to travel through the region is by a car or a minibus. For further information follow the link below:
https://bit.ly/2nH6M35

Moreover, there is an airport in Ambrolauri so you can also get there by plane which departs from the regional airport of Natakhtari (very close to Tbilisi). For further details, follow the link below:
https://ticket.vanillasky.ge/en/tickets

- **Highlights of Racha-Lechkhumi – Kvemo Svaneti**

The nature of Racha-Lechkhumi – Kvemo Svaneti is exceptionally beautiful and is considered to be one of the most impressive regions in Georgia. Due to the fact that the area is mountainous and some villages are not developed that much, it is sometimes quite hard to get proper directions to reach particular places. For that reason, it is highly recommended to go on a tour offered by various companies to better explore the area.

Even though, this travel guide will provide information about several must-see places in the region.

Racha-Lechkhumi

- **<u>Ambrolauri</u>** – located on both banks of the River Rioni, Ambrolauri is the regional capital of Racha-Lechkhumi and Kvemo Svaneti. The town has had a role as a wine route; therefore, the massive bottle of Khvanchkara stands in the center of Ambrolauri.

- **<u>Oni</u>** – another main town in Racha-Lechkhumi region which is situated in a deep gorge on the left bank of River Rioni.

Basically, when you travel to Racha-Lechkhumi, you should either stay in Ambrolauri or Oni since these two towns make it possible to move from one place to another easily. Moreover, these towns are the most developed ones in the region, so you have access to banks, supermarkets, local bazaars, etc. The major highlights of Racha-Lechkhumi are listed below.

- *Shaori Lake* – also referred to as Shaori Reservoir. This is the first landmark that you notice when you enter the region. It is an all-season beautiful lake. The area is quite cool in summer and snowed or even frozen in winter. Since mixed forests surround the area, the lake is awe-inspiring during autumn months when the woods are represented in different colors reflected in the lake. This is an excellent place for a picnic, fishing, or camping with friends and family.

- *Tskhra (9) Jvari* – meaning Nine Crosses. People sometimes refer to this place as "one step away from heaven." The area is quite challenging to reach since you have to hike approximately 3km of rocky paths. At the top of the mountain, you will see nine crosses and more importantly, an impressive view of nature. The place is usually partially or even fully covered in fog, so you have a feeling that you are standing on the clouds. Try to pick a sunny day to visit the place.

- *Nikortsminda Cathedral* – one of the most important highlights of the region located in Nikortsminda, a village near Ambrolauri. It is a Georgian Orthodox Church built in 1010-1013 during the reign of Bagrat III. There is a bell-tower next to the cathedral which was built in the late 19th century. The frescoes on the inner church walls date back to the 17h century. The Nikortsminda Cathedral is in the list of a UNESCO World Heritage Site.

- *Barakoni Cathedral* – also referred to as Barakoni Church of Mother of God. It is an Orthodox church located in the village of Tsesi, near Ambrolauri. The church was commissioned by Rostom Eristavi (local lord) of Racha in 1753. Situated on a top of a steep cliff, the cathedral opens the view of River Rioni which joins the River Lukhuni right below the mountain.

- *Mravaldzali Saint George Church* – located in Zemo

(Upper) Racha, the place opens the view of all surrounding areas and mountains. The church dates back to the 11th century and exceptionally beautiful during snowy winter days due to its white color.

- *Krikhi* – a small village near Ambrolauri. Very beautiful place for hiking or camping with friends and family. One of the most important facility is Luxury Tent Glamping which provides quite impressive services. For more information, you can follow the link below:
- https://www.glampingeorgia.com/

- *Shovi* – balneological-climatic and health resort located 30km away from Oni. It is a wonderful place for picnics, but due to the chilly weather even during summer months, it is not recommended to stay in nature at night. Suited on 1650m above sea level, it belongs to the list of semi-alpine resorts. It comprises one of the most beautiful lakes, Udziro Lake.

- **Accommodation**

Popular Hotels in/near Ambrolauri
Silovani
42 Kostava Str.
+995 551 50 95 15
hotel.silovani@yahoo.com
From 70 GEL

. . .

Metekhara
2 Gamsakhurdia Str.
+995 596 22 12 21
hotelmetekhararacha@gmail.com
From 70 GEL

Mero
Village Nikortsminda
+995 557 25 89 24
gurgenidzeana00@gmail.com
From 40 GEL

Garemo
Sadmeli, Ambrolauri
+995 598 89 08 33
https://bit.ly/2nAyVck
From 25 GEL

Popular Hotels in Oni

e

Orion Hotel
Aghmashenebeli Square
+995 595 14 64 77
www.hotelorion.ge/oni
From 80 GEL

EKE-House in Forest
62 Stalini Str.
+995 557 69 69 79
https://bit.ly/2ocJ7rB

From 25 GEL

Fazisi
Utsera Str.
+995 599 53 63 52
https://bit.ly/2mDEeaS
From 20 GEL

Popular Hotels in Shovi

HOTEL: ADDRESS

**Phone Number
Website
Price Range**

Sunset Shovi
Oni, Shovi, 3600
+995 577 90 19 01
+995 571 76 88 55
www.sunsetshovi.ge/en
From 245 GEL

Guest House Gola Shovi
Oni, Shovi, 3600
+995 577 30 31 94
+995 577 30 52 90
https://bit.ly/2nAX0j6
From 30 GEL

- **Important Contacts**

- *Ambrolauri Tourist Information Center*
- Address: Vazha-Pshavela Str. 17, Ambrolauri
- Tel: +995 595 00 36 56
- E-mail: ticambrolauri@gmail.com
- Website: https://georgia.travel; www.gnta.ge

5
____

GURIA

- **Geography and Demographics**

Guria is a region in the western part of Georgia, bordered by the eastern end of the Black Sea to the west, Samegrelo to the north-west, Imereti to the north, Samtskhe-Javakheti to the east, and Adjara to the south.

Guria, the regional capital of which is Ozurgeti, is divided into 4 entities which are the following: City of Ozurgeti, Ozurgeti Municipality, Lanchkhuti Municipality, and Chokhatauri Municipality.

The region has a population of approximately 113,000 people. 98% of the whole population is ethnic Georgian (mainly Gurulebi, or Gurians), while 1% is ethnic Armenian and the remaining 1% is composed of Russians and Ossetians.

- **Climate and Seasonality**

Summers in the region of Guria are quite long, warm, muggy, wet, and partially cloudy while the winters are short, dry, and mostly clear.

The Summer season typically lasts for about 4 months (from

June 2nd to September 22nd) with an average daily temperature higher than 23.8°C.

The Winter season generally lasts for about 3 months (From December 1st to March 14th) with an average daily temperature below 12.7°C.

Considering the statistical data regarding the weather in Guria, the best time of year to visit the region varies from early June to mid-September. The number of tourists visiting Guria reaches a peak in the first week of July since tourists generally prefer bright, rainless days with temperatures between 18°C and 27°C.

- **Religion and Language**

The majority of the population (86%) in Guria identifies themselves as Orthodox Christians while some ethnic minorities follow Islam.

The language spoken in Guria is Gurian dialect of the Georgian language.

- **How to get to Guria**

To get to the region, you can travel via train from Tbilisi to Ozurgeti. Ticket prices start from approximately $3 and go up to $12. To check further details, follow the link below:
https://ticket.railway.ge/

Another option to reach Ozurgeti is to take a minibus from Tbilisi, Didube Bus Terminal, which costs approximately $5. For further information follow the link below:
https://bit.ly/2nH6M35

- **Highlights of Guria**

Due to the proximity of mountains and sea, the nature of the region along with its climate is diverse. It comprises mountainous areas as well as sea-side resorts.

- **Bakhmaro** – referred to as small heaven on earth. It is an alpine resort situated at 2,000m altitude. The resort offers fantastic curing conditions due to the fresh air of the hills.

- *- Breathtaking Sunrise/Sunset -* Bakhmaro is well-known for the most beautiful sunrise/sunset views in Georgia. Every tourist must hike up a mountain to enjoy a stunning sunrise or a sunset.

- *- Horse-Racing –* local people from Guria were the first to open country's door to European and American nations with their horseback-riding skills. Even though the tradition of horse-racing was wiped out from Gurian's interests, the old tradition was revived at the beginning of the 21st century. Since then, every August the 19th (the day of Transfiguration of Christ), there are various festivals, and different horse-riders from distinct regions of Georgia participate in a race.

- **Ozurgeti** – being the capital of the region of Guria, Ozurgeti is a regional center of tea and hazelnut processing. Most of the town is located between the Bzhuzhi and Natanebi rivers. The climate in the city is Humid Subtropical with significant rainfall throughout the year. Best time to visit the place is late spring, summer, or early autumn.

- - *Gomis Mta* – meaning Gomi Mountain in English. It is a resort which is distinguished with its panoramic views of mountains, beautiful sunset and sunrise, and various stunning summer cottages of the alpine zone. The resort is mostly visited in late spring or summer months. It is an excellent place for hiking and camping as well as off-roading.

- **Coastal Cities of Guria** – along with the mountain resorts, Guria is rich in seaside resorts, including Ureki, Shekvetili, and Grigoleti. These resorts are characterized by magnetic sands loaded with iron particles which are favorable for cardiovascular and respiratory systems. If you get bored by sunbathing at a beach, you can easily get to a theme park Tsitsinatela (located in Shekvetili) which offers 40 distinct attractions.

- **Accommodation**

Popular Hotels in Ozurgeti

Hotel Sam
    25 Guramishvili Str.
    +995 496 23 11 26
    www.hotelsam.ge

From 60 GEL

Brooks
    17 Guria Str.
    +995 593 64 69 99
    https://bit.ly/2nCLlAi
    From 40 GEL

Hotel Elene 1
    7 Kaprovani Str.
    +995 593 57 49 09
    gugadarchiaguga@outlook.com
    From 40 GEL

Popular Hotels in Ureki

HOTEL: ADDRESS

**Phone Number
Website
Price Range**

    Kolkhida Resort & Spa
    117 Takaishvili Str. 6000
    +995 599 20 54 45
    www.kolkhida.ge
    From 300 GEL
    Mirage
    Ekvtime Takaishvili Str. 3rd Turn, 0192
    +995 593 33 72 29
    https://bit.ly/2nB1YfK
    From 150 GEL

Apollo Cottages
Ekvtime Takaishvili Str. 3522
+995 593 33 72 29
https://bit.ly/2nCooNP
From 100 GEL

Popular Hotels in Grigoleti
Ippa S Plaza
61 Bakhmaro Str.
+995 551 68 75 75
https://bit.ly/2nGZKLG
From 80 GEL

Central
Bakhmaro Str.
+995 595 33 50 38
https://bit.ly/2oftnEd
From 50 GEL

Akhali Talga
Grigoleti Square
+995 597 92 64 42
https://bit.ly/2okdGMb
From 30 GEL

Popular Hotels in Shekvetili

Paragraph Resort & Spa Shekvetili
Highway E70, Shekvetili Beach, 3521
+995 32 299 99 00
www.paragraphhotels.com/en

From 550 GEL

Resolute Shekvetili Hotel
    Highway E70, Shekvetili Beacj, 3526
    +995 551 62 32 32
    www.resolutehotels.com
    From 350 GEL

Black Sea Riviera Hotel
    Ozurgeti-Natanebi-Shekvetili, 3521
    +995 599 34 67 47
    www.riviera.ge
    From 300 GEL

Simple Pleasures Shekvetili
    Shekvetili-Kaprovani, Natanebi, 3521
    +995 558 99 98 22
    www.simplepleasures.holiday/
    From 280 GEL

Olimp
    Shekvetili Beach
    +995 591 15 51 11
    https://bit.ly/2mMKDQY
    From 180 GEL

Michel
    Shekvetili Beach, Zone I
    +995 593 33 13 13
    https://bit.ly/2ocIWMW
    From 100 GEL

. . .

MAI

Shekvetili Beach
+995 555 79 38 70
https://bit.ly/2mNOM7g
From 30 GEL

6

AUTONOMOUS REPUBLIC OF ADJARA

- **Geography and Demographics**

The Autonomous Republic of Adjara is a historical, political-administrative, and geographic region located in the south-western corner of Georgia. Adjara lies on the southeastern coast of the Black Sea near the foot of the Lesser Caucasus Mountains. The region is bordered by Turkey to the south, Guria to the north, and Samtskhe-Javakheti to the east.

Majority of Adjara's territory either comprises hills or mountains. Forests cover about 60% of the whole area.

The population of Adjara is approximately 349,000. Most of the community consists of Georgian people while there are several ethnic minorities, including Russians, Armenians, Greeks, Abkhaz, and others.

- **Climate and Seasonality**

Adjara is well known for its humid climate (specifically along the coastal regions) due to the border with the Black Sea. Adjara is identified as the region both in Georgia and in the Caucasus receiving the highest amounts of precipitation. Even though prolonged rainy weather is characteristic to the area, there is plentiful sunshine during late spring, summer, and early autumn months.

Average summer temperature in the lowland areas varies from 22 to 24°C while in the highlands the temperature is between 17 and 21°C.

Average winter temperature along the coast is between 4 and 6°C, and in the interior areas and mountains, it varies from -3 to 2°C. The average winter temperature in some of the high peaks of Adjara varies from -8 to -7°C.

Since Adjara is a coastal region comprising seaside resorts, the best time to travel to the area is summer or early autumn (till mid-September).

- **Religion and Language**

The Georgian population of Adjara region had been typically identified as "Muslim Georgians" until the 1926 Soviet Census. Nowadays, 70% of the whole population of Adjara identify themselves as Orthodox Christians, while there are remaining Sunni Muslim communities (mainly in the Khulo district). There are several minor religious groups, including Armenian Christians.

People in Adjara speak the Adjarian dialect of the Georgian language.

- **How to get to Adjara**

To get to the region, you can take a minibus at the Didube Bus Terminal ($4), or Bus Terminal "Okriba" ($7). For further details check the link below:

https://bit.ly/2nH6M35

Moreover, you can also travel by train to reach various seaside resorts of Adjara. Follow the link below to check the schedules and further details:

https://ticket.railway.ge/

Another way to get to the region is via airplane from Tbilisi or Kutaisi to Batumi. Follow the link below to get additional information regarding the fights:

https://bit.ly/2nGO8bz

- **Highlights of Adjara**

Adjara is the most popular holiday destination in Georgia. It is considered as one of the most beautiful and stunning regions of the country. The area includes several coastal resorts which are appreciated not only by local people but also by tourists from various countries. Adjara is particularly interesting for tourists admiring pristine and unaltered nature.

Adjara is home to the picturesque beaches of Batumi, Mtsvane Kontskhi (meaning Green Cape in English), Kvariati, Gonio, Kobuleti, Tsikhisdziri, and Sarpi (border village). These beach towns offer high-quality infrastructure and fresh air.

- **Batumi** – being the capital city of the Autonomous Republic of Adjara it is the 3rd largest city of Georgia. It is often called "the pearl of the Black Sea." Batumi remains a hub of architectural innovations since the beginning of the 20th century.

- - *Old Batumi* – considered as one of the oldest cities in Georgia. The most historical part is stretched between the Boulevard and the seaport. The area comprises peculiar building facades and balconies.

- - *Batumi Boulevard* – 7km long seaside boardwalk,

which is decorated with bungalows, café-lounges, restaurants, various attractions for children, benches, sculptures, and dancing fountains making the boulevard one of the city's most appealing tourist destinations.

- *Piazza Batumi* – housing several hotels, cafes, and restaurants, Piazza Batumi is considered to be one of the most beautiful squares in the country. The square occasionally hosts different events and concerts by famous Georgian or foreign performers.

- *Batumi Dolphinarium* – located on the 6th of May Park, Batumi Dolphinarium is considered as one of the most visited tourist destinations in the city. The show is offered in 3 languages (English, Georgian, Russian) and is quite affordable. The Dolphinarium is surrounded by an aquarium, zoo, and amusement attractions for children. Moreover, you can also go on a boat tour on Nurigeli Lake from the same park.

- *Batumi Cable Car* – 2km long cable car which links Batumi's waterfront to the Argo Entertainment Center Development on Anuria Mountain. The cable car opens stunning views of the town, the Black Sea, and nearby mountains. The Argo Entertainment center houses several restaurants, cafes, shops, open-air halls, and roof terraces.

- *- Batumi Botanical Garden* – comprises a wide variety of flora from phytogeographic areas, including East Asia, New Zealand, North and South Americas, the Himalayas, Australia, Mexico, the Mediterranean, and the Caucasian Humid Subtropics. Covers the area of 111 hectares. Visitors can choose between the options to wander by foot or rent a cart.

- *- Makhuntseti Waterfall* – located near the town od Keta, it is an excellent place for picnics. The waterfall is surrounded by the ancient arched stone Makhuntseti Bridge, Adjarian Wine House, and private wine cellars which can also be visited by tourists.

- **Food and Entertainment**

Bars, Lounges, and Night Clubs in Batumi
Hookah Bar Po-Krasote
6 Mazniashvili Str.
+995 558 54 52 55
1PM – 2AM
https://www.facebook.com/po.krasote.batumi/
Iveria Beach
Miracle Park (In front of the Alphabet Tower)
+995 422 29 99 91
N/A
https://www.facebook.com/IveriaBeach
Jasmine Lounge Bar
28 Rustaveli Str. (Sheraton Batumi)
+995 422 22 90 00
8AM – 1AM

http://www.sheratonbatumi.com/restaurants-bars
Conte
Zviad Gamsakhurdia Str. 1/5
+995 555 27 12 12
10AM – 2AM
https://www.facebook.com/contebatumi/
Karaoke Club Mario
Airport Hwy., 124
+995 577 08 24 08
10AM – 2AM
N/A
Take Five
Old Boulevard
+995 595 79 79 35
10AM – 2AM
https://www.facebook.com/takefivebatumi/
Jacky's Cocktail Bar
Akhmed Melashvili Str. 16/5
+995 599 28 38 73
4PM – 2AM
https://www.facebook.com/Jackys-Cocktail-Bar-12979330137117194/
Wadim's Home
16 Noe Jordania Str.
+995 555 41 73 30
10AM – 2AM
N/A
Karaoke Club Caruso
13 Zubalashvili Str.
+995 597 20 62 03
10PM – 7AM
N/A
Sky Lounge & Disco
Cross of Kobaladze and Mtsvane Str.
+995 579 99 53 33
10PM – 3AM

N/A
Sector 26
Old Boulevard
+995 555 70 70 66
10PM – 7AM
https://www.facebook.com/BatumiSector26/
Discorioum Night Club
11 Ninoshvili Str.
+995 422 27 55 25
N/A
N/A
Soho Lounge Batumi
Old Boulevard, Sector 27
+995 592 91 91 91
N/A
https://www.facebook.com/NewSohoBatumi/

Top Restaurants for Traditional Cuisine in Batumi
Retro
Zurab Gorgiladze Str. 54/62
+995 579 51 17 22
www.retro.ge
Café Laguna
Zurab Gorgiladze Str. 18
+995 422 22 52 12
N/A
Keria
39, 26 May Str.
+995 514 18 82 82
https://www.facebook.com/keria.awesome/
Cerodena
4 Melikishvili Str.
+995 558 31 18 03
http://www.infobatumi.ge/en/guide/cerodena/
Leuville
Zurab Gorgiladze Str. 1

+995 593 08 60 86
https://www.facebook.com/LeuvilleBatumi/
Porto Franco
40 K. Gamsakhurdia Str.
+995 422 27 62 22
https://www.facebook.com/RestaurantPortoFranco/

1. **Accommodation**

Popular Hotels in Batumi
Colosseum Marina
16 Sherif Khimshiashvili Str.
+995 42 224 44 00
www.colosseummarina.ge

From 400 GEL
Radisson Blu
1 Egnate Ninoshvili Str.
+995 42 225 55 55
www.radissonhotels.com

From 300 GEL
Hilton Batumi
40 Rustaveli Ave.
+995 42 222 22 99
www.hilton.com
From 300 GEL
Wyndham Batumi
33 Mamed Abashidze Str.
+995 42 222 22 00
www.wyndhamhotels.com
From 300 GEL

·   ·   ·

Mardi Plaza
    5 Chavchavadze Str.
    +995 42 222 29 29
    www.mardiplaza.ge
    From 250 GEL

Divan Suites
    Kostava/Zviad Gamsakhurdia Str. 5/13
    +995 42 225 55 22
    www.divan.com.tr
    From 250 GEL

Sheraton Batumi
    28 Rustaveli Str.
    +995 42 222 90 00
    www.sheratonbatumi.ge
    From 190 GEL

Era Palace
    77 Zurab Gorgiladze Str.
    +995 577 50 45 06
    www.erapalace.ge
    From 180 GEL

Piazza Inn
    20 Vakhtang Gorgasali Str.
    +995 32 260 15 36
    www.piazza.ge
    From 170 GEL

Metro City Euphoria
    6000 Lech and Maria Kaczynski Str.

+995 514 02 02
www.metrocity.ge
From 160 GEL

Aisi
153 Gorgasali Str.
+995 568 32 00 99
www.hotelaisi.ge
From 160 GEL

Galogre
8 Vakhtang Gorgasali Str.
+995 592 75 80 00
www.hotelgalogre.ge
From 150 GEL

Hulus
20 Tamar Mepe Str.
+995 595 95 78 68
N/A
From 120 GEL

Orbi Residence
2 Kobaladze Str.
+995 551 15 50 86
N/A
From 80 GEL

House Sun Hostel
24 Lermontovi Str.
+995 558 11 11 89
N/A

From 50 GEL

Popular Hotels in/near Kobuleti

Castello Mare
Tsikhisdziri 6100
+995 422 21 28 28
www.castellomare.com
From 300 GEL

Georgia Palace
275 D. Aghmashenebeli Ave.
+995 577 24 24 25
www.gph.ge
From 250 GEL

Pearl of the Sea
42 Tamar Mepe Str.
+995 555 04 55 00
www.pearlkobuleti.com
From 200 GEL

Condori
280 D. Aghmashenebeli Ave.
+995 599 15 03 00
www.sastumroebi.ge/condori-en
From 140 GEL

Guest House Shine
355 D. Aghmashenebeli Ave.
+995 555 42 20 49

www.sastumroebi.ge/hotel-shine-kobuleti-en
From 140 GEL

Guest House Ponto
    386 D. Aghmashenebeli Ave.
    +995 593 33 33 44
    www.sastumroebi.ge/hotel-sastumro-ponto-en
    From 100 GEL

Hotel ILIA
    66 D. Aghmashenebeli Ave. (House #1)
    +995 577 09 24 64
    www.sastumroebi.ge/sastumro-hotel-ilia
    From 100 GEL

Guest House Saba
    369 D. Aghmashenebeli Ave.
    +995 599 91 00 04
    www.booking.com/hotel/ge/guest-house-saba
    From 45 GEL

Popular Hotels in Gonio

Gonio Inn
    5 Andria Pirveltsodebuli Str.
    +995 598 71 16 16
    www.gonioinn.ge
    From 160 GEL

Mgzavrebi Gonio
    15 Andria Pirveltsodebuli Str., III Alley

+995 555 50 19 05
www.mgzavrebi.ge
From 150 GEL

Citro Villa
65B Svimon Kananeli Str.
+995 592 77 91 79
www.facebook.com/CitroVillaGonio/
From 60 GEL

Popular Hotels in Kvariati

Apart Hotel Kvariati
112 A. Apakidze Str.
+995 599 03 33 22
jabamateshvili@gmail.com
From 170 GEL

Temo
120 Andria Pirveltsodebuli Str.
+995 557 23 87 77
teo.qoqoladze@yahoo.com
From 70 GEL

Royal House
42 Ionae Iazadze Str.
+995 579 02 95 12
gogitidzesulxani2@gmail.com
From 50 GEL

Popular Hotels in Chakvi

. . .

Talga
    28 Ninoshvili Str.
    +995 599 51 18 04
    https://bit.ly/2mDUuIX
    From 70 GEL

Ilia
    66 Aghmashenebeli Str.
    +995 577 09 24 64
    https://bit.ly/2mMi8mk
    From 40 GEL

Sweet Home
    4a Dumbadze Str.
    +995 574 71 00 53
    https://bit.ly/2mMisl2
    From 20 GEL

Popular Hotels in Sarpi

Sunrise Sarpi Cottage
    1 Shavi Zgva Str.
    +995 514 16 10 10
    https://bit.ly/2mQ8Vtc
    From 80 GEL

Black Sea Hotel
    28 Andria Pirveltsodebuli Str.
    +995 599 15 44 37
    https://bit.ly/2mDlIzq

From 80 GEL

Silvia
    5 Sarpi Str.
    +995 577 68 96 47
    https://bit.ly/2nCOMXI
    From 40 GEL

7

IMERETI

- **Geography and Demographics**

Imereti is a region located in the western part of Georgia. The region is bordered by Likhi Range to the east, river Tskhenistrkali to the west, Caucasus mountains to the north and Persati (Meskheti mountains) to the south.

The total area of the region is $6,475km^2$ while $2,500km^2$ of the territory is covered with forests (primarily spread across the mountainous landscape).

Imereti is divided into two parts, Upper and Lower Imereti. The region consists of 12 administrative-territorial units which are the following: Kutaisi (city; the regional capital of Imereti), Municipalities of Baghdati, Vani, Zestafoni, Terjola, Samtredia, Sachkhere, Tkibuli, Chiatura, Tskaltubo, Kharagauli, and Khoni.

Traditionally, Imereti is an agricultural region known for its grapes and mulberries. Several towns and regional centers are also known for the production of manganese (Chiatura), coal mining (Tkibuli), and metal production (Zestafoni).

According to statistical data from 2014, the population of Imereti is approximately 534,000. Most of the community is Georgian (99%) while there are some Armenians, Azeris, and other ethnic groups.

- **Climate and Seasonality**

Majority of the area of Imereti is located in the humid subtropical climate zone. Even though the influence of the sea is weak in lower and middle mountain regions, the climate is still humid.

Winters in the region are cold with an average temperature of 5°C in January, while summers are quite hot and dry with an average temperature of 30°C in August. The maximum temperature during the summer months has reached 38°C.

Best seasons to visit the region would be March-May or September-November since the temperatures are quite mild.

- **Religion and Language**

Majority of the population in Imereti is Orthodox Christian while there are still some other religious groups identified within the society.

People in Imereti speak in the dialect of Georgian language called "Imeruli" dialect.

- **How to get to Imereti**

To reach the region, you can take a minibus from one of the bus stations in Tbilisi. For detailed information, follow the link provided below:

https://bit.ly/2nH6M35

Moreover, you can also travel by train. To check the schedules and other details, please follow the website below:

https://ticket.railway.ge/

Along with that, you can also travel via plane to reach Kutaisi International Airport.

- **Highlights of Imereti**

The region's uniqueness is defined by the geographical location, climate, abundance of the historical and natural environment, and rich cultural traditions. Lots of tourists from around the world are attracted to the mountainous areas and landscapes of the Imereti region.

- **<u>Kutaisi</u>** – being one of the oldest and most important cities in Georgia, it is located 221km away from Tbilisi. The town offers various ancient cultural landmarks for the local people as well as tourists to explore.

- *- Sataplia Nature Reserve* – meaning "place of honey" in English. The name was derived from the tradition of collecting honey from the bees inhabiting the small reserve in Tskaltubo (12km away from Kutaisi). The reserve is famous for the presence of dinosaur footprints and speleothems. The area comprises a cave (900m long, 10m high, 12m wide), a museum, different points that open a precious view of nature, glass walkways with a great view below, as well as cafés and small restaurants.

- *- Prometheus Cave* – also referred to as Kohistani Cave. The name was derived from a Caucasian myth of Amirani according to which Amirani was punished for making the gods angry and was chained somewhere inside the cave while eagles ate him. Located nearby Tskaltubo (20km away from Kutaisi), was discovered in 1984. The cave features breathtaking examples of stalagmites, stalactites, cave pearls, lakes and petrified waterfalls which are millennia old. Even though the cave is one of the largest caves in Georgia, only 10% of the whole territory is accessible to visitors.

- - *Bagrati Cathedral* – built in the 11th century, it is considered as a jewel of medieval architecture. It represents one of the most significant religious sites in Georgia. The cathedral was named after King Bagrat III. The cathedral is listed as UNESCO World Heritage Site.

- - *Gelati Monastery* – located near Bagrati Cathedral, was built in the early 12th century by King David Aghmashenebeli. The monastery includes the burial site of King David. When you reach the monastery, there are several local tour guides offering 60-70-minute tours inside the building so that you can learn more about the design, history, mission, structure, or roles.

- **Tskaltubo** – spa resort located about 10km away from Kutaisi. You can simply take a minibus N30 or N34 from Kutaisi center which costs approximately $0.5. The minibus departs from 8 AM to 7 PM every 20 or 30 minutes.
- The town served as one of the most popular spa resorts in Soviet Georgia, but after the fall of the Soviet Union, the sanatorium in Tskaltubo lost its function. Despite that, the abandoned sanatorium is still an incredible building worth visiting.

- **Sairme** – balneological-climatic resort located in Baghdati Municipality. Situated on the northern slope of Meskheti Range, it is suited on 950m above Sea Level. The resort features a sanatorium, resort, and a polyclinic. It is a great place just to relax and enjoy fresh air along with mountain views.

- **Chiatura** – known for high amounts of manganese ore which plays a key role in the development of the city.

- *Katskhis Sveti* – meaning Katskhi Pillar in English. Located in the village of Katskhi near the town of Chiatura, it is a 40m high pillar with visible church ruins on top of it. Katskhis Sveti has been associated with the Pillar of Life and a symbol of the True Cross for the local people.

- **Okatse Canyon** – located in the village Gordi, Khoni Municipality. The trip starts with the 2-3 hour long pedestrian route passes which pass through Dadiani ancient forests. The track also includes hanging trail of 780m length. The final stop of the trip is the panoramic view of mesmerizing nature. Entrance for the children under 6 years is free, for individuals from 6 to 18 is 5.5 GEL, for Georgian citizens above 18 is 9.20 GEL, and for citizens of other countries above 18 is 17.25 GEL. Moreover, you can even arrange a civil marriage signing ceremony which costs 100 GEL.

- **<u>Vani Archeological Museum</u>** – houses several important ancient Georgian artifacts. It is considered that one of the principal Colchian towns was located at the territory of Zeda (upper) Vani. By visiting the museum who can learn more about the Chokhi culture.

- **<u>Akaki Tsereteli House Museum in Skhvitori</u>** – by visiting the house-museum you can learn more about the famous Georgian poet Akaki Tsereteli. The museum features his and his ancestors' personal items, which include 19th-century furniture from Italy, France, and Germany, as well as utensils, library, and manuscripts.

- **Accommodation**

Popular Hotels in Kutaisi

Best Western Kutaisi
   11 Grishashvili Str.
   +995 32 219 71 00
   www.bestwestern.com
   From 250 GEL

West Tower Hotel
   44 Z. Gamsakhurdia Str.
   +995 599 76 65 99
   https://bit.ly/2on82sH

From 180 GEL

Bagrati 1003
   2a Tsereteli Str.
   +995 555 69 30 30
   www.bagrati1003.ge
   From 150 GEL

Hotel Eurica
   12 Kazbegi Str.
   +995 591 11 94 69
   https://bit.ly/2ooHiIt
   From 90 GEL

Hotel Dimasi
   9 Mari Brosse Str.
   +995 599 50 70 54
   www.hoteldimasi.ge
   From 80 GEL

Family Hotel
   40 Shota Rustaveli Ave.
   +995 599 08 72 04
   https://bit.ly/2nKAqED
   From 50 GEL

Popular Hotels in Tskaltubo

HOTEL: ADDRESS

Phone Number

Website
Price Range

Prometheus
11 Rustaveli Str.
+995 555 30 54 91
https://bit.ly/2mQKOL8
From 120 GEL

Vita Garden
7 Samakashvili Str.
+995 555 78 88 11
https://bit.ly/2mGQs2v
From 40 GEL

Oda
15 Kazbegi Str.
+995 555 98 08 83
https://bit.ly/2nKBCb5
From 15 GEL

Popular Hotels in Sairme
Sairme Hotels & Resorts
1000, Sairme
+995 32 240 45 45
https://bit.ly/2nI4RM0
From 300 GEL

Best Western Sairme Resort
Bagdati District, Resort Sairme
+995 32 240 45 46
https://bit.ly/2m5DhYx
From 250 GEL

. . .

Hotel Maia
  Central Sairme
  +995 579 24 44 11
  https://bit.ly/2mPSugE
  From 80 GEL

8

KAKHETI

Sighnaghi – the City of Love

• Geography and Demographics

Kakheti is a region in the eastern part of the country formed in the 1990s from the historical province of Kakheti and the small mountainous province of Tusheti. The area is bordered by the Russian Federation to the northeast, Azerbaijan to the southeast, and Mtskheta-Mtianeti and Kvemo Kartli to the west.

The region with the total area of 11,311km^2 has been traditionally subdivided into 4 parts which are the following:

• Shida (Inner) Kakheti – to the east of Tsiv-Gombori

mountain range (along the right bank of the Alazani River);
- Gare (Outer) Kakheti – along the middle Iori River basin;
- Kiziq'I – between the Alazani and the Iori rivers;
- Thither Area – on the left bank of the Alazani River.

Furthermore, the region is divided into 8 municipalities, including Telavi, Akhmeta, Gurjaani, Kvareli, Dedoplistrkaro, Lagodekhi, Sagarejo, and Sighnaghi. The regional capital of Kakheti is the city of Telavi.

Kakheti has a population of approximately 314,700 people. Most populated cities/municipalities of Kakheti are Gurjaani, Telavi, Lagodekhi, Kvareli, Akhmeta, and Sighnaghi. 85.2% of the population is ethnic Georgian followed by 10.2% Azeris, and 0.7% Armenians. The remaining percentage is divided among minority ethnic groups.

- **Climate and Seasonality**

Kakheti comprises diverse climate zones which are provided below:

- Humid Subtropical Climate – characteristic to Sagarejo, Gurjaani, Kvareli, Akhmeta, Karajala;
- Hot-Humid Continental Climate – distinctive to Telavi, Duisi, Kakabeti, Ninotsminda, Khashmi;
- Warm Humid Continental Climate – characteristic to Patardzeuli, Omalo, Zemo Kandaura, Dedisperuli, Mariandjvari;
- Subarctic Climate – Diklo Khakhabo, Dano, Bochorma, Dochu.

Best season for tourists to visit the region can be considered to be between spring, summer, and autumn since the weather is quite warm even during spring and autumn months.

- **Religion and Language**

People living in Kakheti region predominantly follow Orthodox Christianity (86.7% of the total population). 12.3% of society is identified as Muslim. Moreover, there are small groups of Armenian Christians within the region, along with people with no religion or other religious beliefs.

- **How to get to Kakheti**

You can simply take a minibus to reach different towns of the region of Kakheti. For further details, please follow the link below:
https://bit.ly/2nH6M35

- **Highlights of Kakheti**

Since Kakheti is not that far away from Tbilisi, it is one of the most visited places in Georgia. The region is famous for its breathtaking landscapes, including snowy peaks and curving passes, traditions regarding wine production in Kvevri, etc.

Kakheti features several important monasteries and cathedrals which are worth visiting if you are traveling in this area.

- **David Gareji** – located in the desert that borders with Azerbaijan, it is a complex of rock-hewn cave monasteries dating back to the 6th century. Since part of the complex is located in the Agstafa rayon of Azerbaijan, the area has become the subject to a border dispute between Georgia and Azerbaijan. The area features some of the oldest human habitations in the region as well as various protected animal species.

- **Alaverdi Monastery** – 11th-century cathedral is the second tallest religious building in Georgia (after the Holy Trinity Cathedral in Tbilisi). The annual religious event called Alaverdoba is celebrated at this monastery. The local monks make their own wine which is known as Alaverdi Monastery Cellar.

- **Nekresi Monastery** – located in Kvareli, it is considered as the oldest Christian Orthodox church in Georgia which dates back to the 4th. It had been the most essential cultural, political, educational, and spiritual center of the nation in the past. The complex comprises several structures built in different periods. This is the only church in Georgia to which the pig can be sacrificed since according to the legend when Muslims attacked Nekresi, defenders of the monastery let the pigs out make the Muslims leave the cathedral in peace.

- **Gremi Monastery** – located in the Kvareli district, it is a 16th-century monument which features the royal citadel and the church of the Archangels.

- **Bodbe Monastery** – also referred to as the Monastery of Saint Nino at Bodbe. It is located 2km away from Sighnaghi. The monastery is considered among the important religious sites of Georgia. The best way to explore the area is to join private tours and weekend trips offered by various companies or even local travel guides.

- **<u>Estate of Prince Chavchavadze</u>** – palace and gardens of Prince Alexander Chavchavadze who is one of the most influential figures in Georgian history. Located in the village of Tsinandali, the park comprises ancient trees and unique plants, including but not limited to Sequoia, Ginkgo, and Yucca. Moreover, the place also features the winery which is worth visiting.

- **<u>Sighnaghi</u>** – considered as the City of Love by local people. Even though it is one of the smallest towns in Georgia, it is still considered as one of the charming ones with stunning landscapes, cobblestone streets, and pastel-colored houses. In case if you are traveling with your loved one, you can easily get married at the civil ceremony office which is open 24 hours a day for 7 days a week.

- **<u>Telavi</u>** – the regional capital of Kakheti houses several world-famous wineries, castles, art museums, and a theater. It is a perfect place to stop for lunch during the several-day excursions in the region.

- **<u>Luxurious Resorts</u>** – there are several luxury resorts within Kakheti that are worth visiting. Several examples of places for you to relax and enjoy your time in beautiful nature are the following:

- Royal Batoni, Lopota Lake Resort, and Spa, Kvareli Lake, Chateau Mere.

- **Accommodation**

Popular Hotels in Gurjaani

Akhasheni Wine Resort
  Gurjaani District, Village 1502
  +995 32 220 00 11
  www.akhasheniwineresort.com
  From 300 GEL

The Role House
  5 D. Aghmashenebeli, 1500 Gurjaani
  N/A
  https://www.facebook.com/rolehouse/
  From 60 GEL

Buto's House
  Village Arashenda, Gurjaani
  N/A
  https://www.a-hotel.com/georgia/34764-gurjaani/
4987205-1-butos-house/
  From 40 GEL

Popular Hotels in Telavi

Schuchmann Wines Chateau, Villas & SPA
  Kisiskhevi Village, 2200 Telavi

+995 577 50 80 05
www.schuchmann-wines.com
From 300 GEL

Savaneti Eco
Ikalto Village, 2206 Telavi
+995 577 05 60 04
www.savaneti.com
From 200 GEL

Chateau Mere
15 Vardisubani Str., 0145 Telavi
+995 595 99 03 99
www.mere.ge
From 150 GEL

Holiday Inn Telavi
2 Rustaveli Avenue, 2200 Telavi
+995 32 261 11 11
www.facebook.com/pg/HolidayInnTelavi/
From 150 GEL

Hotel HAPO
5 Vardoshvili Str., 2200 Telavi
+995 579 40 00 04
www.facebook.com/HapoComplexTelavi/
From 120 GEL

Alazani Valley Hotel
75 Alazani Ave., 2200 Telavi
+995 595 50 01 55
www.alaznisveli.com.ge/

From 110 GEL

New Telavi
    29 Chavchavadze Ave., 2200 Telavi
    +995 574 78 01 01
    www.hotelnewtelavi.com/
    From 95 GEL

The Wine Hotel Telavi
    Alazani Ave., 2200 Telavi
    +995 579 30 02 92
    N/A
    From 90 GEL

Guglux & Wine Cellar
    8 A. Diunani Str., 2200 Telavi
    +995 571 70 07 07
    https://www.booking.com/hotel/ge/guest-house-guglux.en-
gb.html
    From 80 GEL

Guest House Laghidze
    45 University Str, 2200 Telavi
    N/A
    https://www.a-hotel.com/georgia/34551-telavi/3558492-1-
gest-house-laghidze/
    From 60 GEL

Hotel Classic
    12 Griboedovi Str., 0102 Telavi
    +995 568 82 96 96

https://www.booking.com/hotel/ge/classic-telavi.en-gb.html
From 55 GEL

Popular Hotels in Sighnaghi

Kabadoni Boutique Hotel
1 Tamar Mepe Str.
+995 32 224 04 00
www.kabadoni.ge
From 350 GEL

Galavnis Kari
38 Mosashvili Str.
+995 595 46 98 87
www.galavniskari.ge
From 150 GEL

Abramichi
29 Gorgasali Str.
+995 595 61 16 55
https://bit.ly/2mG6mKx
From 100 GEL

9

SAMTSKHE-JAVAKHETI

- **Geography and Demographics**

Samtskhe-Javakheti is a region in the southern part of Georgia. The area comprises historical Georgian provinces of Meskheti, Javakheti, and Tori. The administrative center of Samtskhe-Javakheti is Akhaltsikhe.

The region, area of which is 6,413km^2, is bordered by Adjara to the west, Guria, and Imereti to the North, Shida Kartli and Kvemo Kartli to the northeast and east, and Armenia and Turkey to the south and southwest.

Several critical pipelines and railway pass through Samtskhe-Javakheti, including Baku-Tbilisi-Ceyhan Oil Pipeline, South Caucasus Natural Gas Pipeline, and Kars-Tbilisi-Baku Railway.

Populated areas of the region include 5 cities (Akhaltsikhe, Akhalkalaki, Borjomi, Vale, Ninotsminda), 7 "dabas" which are the settlements categorized in Georgia (Bakuriani, Bakurianis Andeziti, Tsagveri, Akhaldaba, Adigeni, Abastumani, Aspindza), and 258 villages.

According to the data collected in 2017, the population of Samtskhe Javakheti is 160,504. 50.52% of the whole community is Armenian, 48.28% is Georgian, 0.44% is Russian, while the rest of the percentage is divided among other ethnic groups

(Greeks, Ossetians, etc.).

The majority of the population is comprised of Armenians due to the country's southern border to the Republic of Armenia. They are mainly concentrated in Akhalkalaki, Ninotsminda, and Akhaltsikhe.

• **Climate and Seasonality**

Samtskhe-Javakheti has two different climatic environments which are the following: warm humid continental climate (characteristic to Akhaltsikhe, Borjomi, Akhalkalaki, Ninotsminda, Vale, etc.) and Subarctic Climate (characteristic to Gandzani, Poka, Azavreti, Tabatskuri, Modega, etc.).

Best time to visit Samtskhe-Javakheti is considered to be late spring, summer, or early autumn since the weather during these months is neither too cold nor too hot. Moreover, tourists interested in winter sports can also visit the region, specifically daba and skiing resort Bakuriani.

• **Religion and Language**

Even though the majority of the population of Samtskhe-Javakheti is Armenian, 45.6% of the whole population identifies themselves as Orthodox Christians followed by 40.3% as Armenian Apostolic. 3.8% of the population is Muslim while the remaining percentage is divided among people with either other religious backgrounds or no religious beliefs.

Armenian is the common language spoken among Armenians while the majority of them also speaks Georgian.

• **How to get to Samtskhe-Javakheti**

You can simply take a minibus from Tbilisi to reach specific cities of the region of Samtskhe-Javakheti. For further details, please visit the website below:

https://bit.ly/2nH6M35

Another option to get to different areas of the region is using a train. To check the schedules or other details follow the link provided below:

https://ticket.railway.ge/

- **Highlights of Samtskhe Javakheti**

The region which was formed in 1995 after the secession of Abkhazia and the conflict in South Ossetia features various historical landmarks and offers exciting activities. Some of the most popular ones will be discussed below.

- **<u>Borjomi</u>** – resort town laying in the stunning gorge with slopes covered in pine forests. The city is well-known for its mineral water of volcanic origin beneficial due to its therapeutic properties.

- *- Borjomi-Kharagauli National Park* – covers more than 85,000 hectares of native forest and alpine meadows. Visitors are allowed to experience the stunning variety of flora and fauna all year round. All the paths within the park are marked and well-arranged. There are various tourist shelters, picnic stops, and camping sites along the routes. Moreover, the park offers visitors hiking, horse riding, biking, snowshoes, educational, and cultural tours.

- *- Borjomi Central Park* – a newly renovated park which is considered as the main sites of the town. The primary water source is located within the park. Moreover, the park comprises various amusement rides. You only need to pay 2 GEL for the whole-day entrance and enjoy the beautiful nature and fresh air.

- - *Cable Car Ride* – you can explore the views over Borjomi by going to the entrance of the Borjomi Central Park to go on a Borjomi cable car ride. The one-way ride which lasts for several minutes costs 5 GEL. It opens a panoramic view of the city surrounded by pine-covered forests.

- **Bakuriani** – situated on the northern slope of the Trialeti Range, it is a skiing resort in the Borjomi district. The area features a diverse variety of alpine slopes and cross-country trails. It is considered as one of the best skiing and snowboarding destinations in Europe.

- **Akhaltsikhe** – a small city located on both banks of the River Potskhovi. The river separates Akhaltsikhe into old and new parts of the city.

- - *Rabati Castle* – fortress was originally established in the 9th century known as the Lomisa Caste, but Ottomans entirely rebuilt it. Rabati means a "fortified place" in the Arabic language. In 2012, the reconstruction of the fortress was finished, and the castle has been considered as a town within the town since then. The area includes a church, mosque, small park, synagogue, several shops, hotels, a history museum, and a civil marriage office. It is one of the most visited places in the region.

- **<u>Abastumani</u>** - mainly known for the Georgian National Astrophysical Observatory located in the city. This is a perfect spot for star-lovers. You can visit the place until 2 AM and enjoy the stunning views of the starry sky.

- **<u>Vardzia Cave</u>** – a very popular cave monastery which dates back to the 12th century. The cave that extends for 500 meters includes 19 layers or cave residences. Moreover, the cave features 6 chapels, a pharmacy, 25 wine cellars, a meeting room, etc. The cave is one of the most exciting destinations in Georgia and worth exploring if you are traveling to the nearby area.

- **<u>Romanov Summer Residence of the Legendary Dynasty</u>** – also referred to as Romanov's Palace or Likani Palace. It is a stunning example of architecture situated in Likani (close to Borjomi). The palace features a unique collection of royal antique items, including tables (from emperor Napoleon, Iranian Sheikh), chairs (assembled by Piotr the First), billiard table, etc. One of the most popular sites at the palace is a private office of Grand Duke which was later occupied by Joseph Stalin.

- **Accommodation**

Popular Hotels in Bakuriani

Snow Plaza
    Nearby 25m Ski Slope
    +995 577 50 30 15
    www.snowplaza.ge
    From 250 GEL
    Mgzavrebi
    1 K. Tsakadze Str.
    +995 599 89 51 51
    www.mgzavrebi.ge
    From 200 GEL
    Villa Park
    25 Rustaveli Str.
    +995 599 75 55 58
    https://www.facebook.com/villaparkbakuriani/
    From 200 GEL
    Crystal SPA
    Didveli, Bakuriani
    +995 595 46 14 61
    https://www.facebook.com/hotelspacrystal/
    From 200 GEL
    Villa Deluxe
    37 K. Tsakadze Str.
    +995 558 83 08 30
    https://www.facebook.com/VillaDeluxeBakuriani/
    From 150 GEL
    Villa Palace
    1 K. Tsakadze Str.
    +995 597 90 11 44
    https://www.facebook.com/VillaPalaceBakuriani/
    From 120 GEL
    Holiday
    Didveli 1, Bakuriani

+995 571 30 82 82
N/A
100 GEL
Orbi Palace
30 Aghmashenebeli Str.
+995 599 03 25 35
https://www.booking.com/hotel/ge/orbi-palace-bakuriani1.html
From 100 GEL
Victoria
94 Aghmashenebeli Str.
+995 595 92 80 80
https://www.facebook.com/victoriahotelandspa/
From 80 GEL

Popular Hotels in Borjomi

Ecorest
27a Meskheti Str.
+995 577 99 00 75
likanipalace@gmail.com
From 250 GEL

Borjomis Kheoba
103 Rustaveli Ave.
+995 0367 22 30 72
www.borjomiskheoba.com
From 250 GEL

Borjomi Palace
9 Gamsakhurdia Str.
+995 32 243 00 31
www.borjomipalace.ge

From 150 GEL

Apartment Diasamidzeebi
    17 Pirosmani Str.
    +995 595 60 50 50
    apartamentdiasamidzeebi@gmail.com
    From 140 GEL

Guest House
    20 G. Saakadze Str.
    +995 577 30 22 20
    baiajanin@gmail.com
    From 50 GEL

Gio's Guest House
    17 G. Saakadze Str.
    +995 598 10 14 32
    Qetevan.tabagari@gmail.com
    From 40 GEL

Merry's House
    Borjomi-Bakuriani Highway
    +995 571 14 13 89
    gogelianimariami@gmail.com
    From 20 GEL

Popular Hotels in Akhaltsikhe

Gino Wellness Rabath
    1 Kharischirashvili Str.
    +995 599 88 09 24

https://www.facebook.com/ginowellnessrabath/
From 200 GEL

Hotel Tiflis
    26 Aspindza Str.
    +995 568 11 11 88
    info@hoteltiflis.ge
    From 100 GEL
    BENI
    5 Kharischirashvili Str.
    +995 555 77 72 00
    nberdzenidze@mail.ru
    From 80 GEL

Rabath
    58 E. Athoneli Str.
    +995 598 41 91 11
    afriamashvili@gmail.com
    From 50 GEL

Zuka's House
    101 Guramishvili Str.
    +995 555 81 41 66
    durglishvilimari@gmail.com
    From 25 GEL

Popular Hotels in Abastumani

Iveria
    19 L. Asatiani Str.
    +995 599 77 88 81
    https://www.facebook.com/AbastumaniIveriaHotel/

From 200 GEL

Abastumani Residence
    10 Paliashvili Str.
    +995 599 18 22 99
    www.abastumaniresidence.ge
    From 160 GEL

Hotel Kapa
    35 Rustaveli Str.
    +995 551 33 22 88
    https://hotelkapaabastumani.business.site/?utm_source=
gmb&utm_medium=referral
    From 100 GEL

Green Hotel
    6 L. Asatiani Str.
    +995 577 14 41 22
    lasha_chagiashvili@yahoo.com
    From 80 GEL

MTSKHETA-MTIANETI

- **Geography and Demographics**

Mtskheta Mtianeti is a region situated in the eastern part of Georgia. The region incorporates historical and geographical provinces as well as administrative municipalities, including Mtiuleti, Khevi, Gudamakari, Dusheti, Mtskheta, Kazbegi, territories of Shida Kartli, etc. Moreover, the region comprises 6 "dabas" including Akhalgori, Zhinvali, Pasanauri, Tianeti, Sioni, and Stepantsminda.

The total area of the region, which includes snowy mountains, beautiful gorges, lakes, alpine valleys, and meadows, is 6,648km^2.

The population of Mtskheta-Mtianeti is 93,900. Most of the population is Georgian (94.5%), followed by Azerbaijanians (2.4%), Ossetians (1.4%), Assyrian People (0.7%), Armenians (0.3%), and Russians (0.3%).

- **Climate and Seasonality**

Even though Mtskheta-Mtianeti has many different climatic environments, it is dominated by Warm Humid Continental Climate (e.g., in Dusheti, Tvalivi, Pasanauri, Sakdrioni, Sioni, etc.). Another climate zone which is quite common through the region is Subarctic Climate (characteristic to Stepantsminda, Arsha, Kanobi, Sno, Sioni, etc.). Last two climate zones that are characteristic to fewer areas are Humid Subtropical (Mtskheta, Naoza, Aghdgomelaantkari, Jighaura, Misaktsieli, etc.) and Hot-Humid Continental (Tsilkani, Dzalisi, Saskhori, Vardisubani, Tsitelsopeli, etc.).

The best time to visit the region can be considered to be late spring, summer, and early autumn, depending on the specific location of interest. In case if you enjoy winter sports, you might want to visit the region during winter months and enjoy skiing or snowboarding in Gudauri.

- **Religion and Language**

Mtskheta, which is the regional center of Mtskheta-Mtianeti, has been the country's spiritual/religious heart since the establishment of Christianity in Georgia in about 327. Throughout the year, lots of religious events are held in various parts of the region.

Majority of the population in Mtskheta-Mtianeti identify themselves as Orthodox Christians while there are some Muslims along with other minority religious groups.

The language spoken in the Mtskheta-Mtianeti region is predominantly Georgian.

- **How to get to Mtskheta-Mtianeti**

Since the region is quite close to Tbilisi, it is relatively easy to reach the cities within Mtskheta-Mtianeti. You can take a bus at the Didube Bus Station. The ride lasts for about 20 minutes. For more information, follow the link below:
https://bit.ly/2nH6M35

- **Highlights of Mtskheta-Mtianeti**

The region unifies the customs and traditions from the past and modern life as well as natural diversity.

- **Gudauri** – considered as the best ski resort in Georgia equipped with high-quality infrastructure and the greatest difference in altitude. The highest point of Gudauri is Mount Sadzele which is 3,307m above the sea level. Another popular destination is the summit Kudebi (3007m above the sea level). You can use Chair Lifts (Doppelmayr, Austria) or a Gondola Line (POMA, France) to ski or snowboard along the southern slopes. In case if you do not have your equipment with you, ski rentals are located in several places: the village of Lower Gudauri and Upper Gudauri (near the Gondola station).

- **Kazbegi** – also known as Stepantsminda. It is a small town close to the Russian border. The area offers stunning hiking routes and fantastic nature. There are various day trips offered by local travel guides which help you to explore the area better.

- - *Gergeti Trinity Church* – dating back to the 14th century, it is located in the village of Gergeti (6km away from Kazbegi). There are several options to get to the cathedral: hike up to the complex (2 hours hike), hire a driver, or rent a horse.

- - *Stepantsminda Historical Museum* – located in the memorial house of the famous Georgian writer Alexander Kazbegi. Along with the library and personal items of the writer, the museum comprises various ethnographic artifacts characteristic to the Khevi region.

- - *Gveleti Waterfall* – located in the village of Gveleti (7km away from Kazbegi), it is a perfect spot for hiking. Gveleti means a "place of snakes" in English. You can get to the waterfall by first driving to the Dariali Gorge from which you can follow a narrow footpath which leads to the stunning Gveleti waterfall.

- - *Devdoraki Glacier* – starting from Kazbegi to the Dariali Gorge, you reach a hiking trail that leads to the glacier. The area opens the precious view of snowy mountain peaks.

- - *Village Juta* – considered as one of the highest settlements (2,200m above the sea level). It is located 24km away from Kazbegi. The chief sight of Juta is the Chaukhi mountain range located near the village.
- - *Khada Gorge* – located near the Russian border, the area is mostly visited by individuals enjoying hiking and mountain climbing. You reach the gorge by passing through the Dariali Gorge where you can see a newly build monastery complex. The length of the footpath is about 17km so try to be well-equipped if you decide to hike in the area.

- **Mtskheta** – listed among the UNESCO World

Heritage Sites. The area has been inhabited since 1,000 BC and once was the capital of the early Kingdom of Iberia. Located 20km away from Tbilisi, it is an excellent place for weekend trips with friends and family.

- - *Svetitskhoveli Cathedral* – dating back to the 11th century, it has served as the religious center of Georgia for hundreds of years. The monastery complex incorporates a church, gate, bell tower, castles, and clerical residences. The cathedral preserves the mantles of Christ and Prophet Elijah. Svetitskhoveli is listed as a UNESCO World Heritage Site.

- - *Jvari Monastery* – dating back to the 6th century, it is a church built on a hill opposite to Mtskheta. The church is included in the list of UNESCO World Heritage Sites.

- - *Shio-Mgvime* – situated on the left bank of the River Mtkvari it is 8km away from Mtskheta. The monastery was constructed in the late 6th century and includes buildings from different time periods, such as a cave church, a bell tower, the church of Saint John the Baptist, The church of Shio and Saint Mary's Assumption cathedral, the Ascension Church, tower, refectory, rock-cut caves, reservoirs, clergy houses. Moreover, the area features a spring as well as a water supply system.

- *- Zedazeni* – complex located on the top of a mountain 6km away from village Saguramo. Zedazeni complex, which includes the Church of Saint John the Baptist, a fortress, and monastic cave cells, is covered in deep forests.

- *- Armazi Fortress* – Armazi constitutes one of the most important fortresses in Georgia due to its scale and age. Current remains of the fortress occupy about 30 hectares of the territory.

- *- Mtskheta State Archeological Museum-Reserve* – includes various archeological artifacts of national as well as international importance. The collection contains a diverse variety of exhibits from the Bronze and late Middle Ages along with different ethnographic pieces.

- *- Ilia Chavchavadze Saguramo State Museum* – complex that includes the residence, auxiliary building, and the family vineyards belonging to the famous Georgian writer Ilia Chavchavadze. The museum features memorial items and manuscripts, along with some portraits.
- *- Jinvali (Zhinvali) Water Reservoir* – also referred to as Zhinvali lake. It is an artificial lake located on the Georgian Military Highway, in Dusheti Municipality. The dam was constructed in the 1980s since Tbilisi

needed an additional water supply. This is a great spot to take pictures and enjoy the fresh air.

- **Accommodation**

Popular Hotels in Gudauri

Carpe Diem Gudauri
    Kazbegi District, 4702 Gudauri
    +995 514 51 07 70
    www.carpediem.ge
    From 250 GEL

Marco Polo
    4702 Gudauri
    +995 591 11 19 00
    www.marcopolo.ge
    From 250 GEL

Edelweiss
    Upper Gudauri, 0103 Gudauri
    +995 592 98 98 92
    www.facebook.com/Hotel-Edelweiss-Gudauri/
    From 250 GEL

Alpina
    S3 Gudauri
    +995 32 200 70 70
    www.hotelalpina.ge
    From 220 GEL

· · ·

Loft
    4702 Gudauri
    +995 557 10 58 58
    www.gudauriloft.ge
    From 200 GEL

Retro
    Upper Gudauri
    +995 599 60 81 80
    www.facebook.com/Gudaurihotelretro/
    From 180 GEL

Gudauri Hut
    S3 Gudauri
    +995 595 93 99 11
    www.gudaurihut.com
    From 170 GEL

Good Aura
    Kazbegi District, 4702 Gudauri
    +995 571 50 30 11
    www.hotelgoodaura.com
    From 150 GEL

Zviad1
    Kvesheti, Gudauri
    +995 599 96 09 39
    Jag500@mail.ru
    From 60 GEL

Popular Hotels in Kazbegi/Sioni

· · ·

Rooms Hotel Kazbegi
    1 Gorgasali Str.
    +995 32 240 00 99
    www.roobshotels.com/kazbegi/
    From 250 GEL

Porta Caucasia Kazbegi
    2 Tergdaleulebi Str.
    +995 32 225 77 70
    www.portacaucasia.com
    From 200 GEL

Hotel Sno Kazbegi
    Village Sno, Kazbegi
    +995 598 70 70 01
    https://bit.ly/2nJw40s
    From 150 GEL

Sioni
    26 L. Larseli Str., Sioni, Kazbegi
    +995 599 78 46 00
    https://bit.ly/2m7Xwov
    From 80 GEL

Starry Night
    Sioni, Kazbegi, 4700
    +995 598 83 25 27
    https://bit.ly/2olsKcl
    From 50 GEL

Popular Hotels in Mtskheta

· · ·

The Balcony
  1 Aghmashenebeli str.
  +995 558 91 95 74
  https://bit.ly/2ooRjW5
  From 160 GEL

Old Capital
  7 Erekle II Str.
  +995 593 63 17 86
  https://bit.ly/2m7YIIv
  From 150 GEL

SANI
  108 Aghmashenebeli Str.
  +995 599 14 16 18
  https://bit.ly/2onhv3d
  From 70 GEL

SHIDA KARTLI

• Geography and Demographics

Shida Kartli also referred to as Inner Kartli, is an administrative region in the eastern part of Georgia. The administrative center of the region is Gori, largest city of the region. The total area of the region is 5,729km^2.

The northern part of the region, called Java, as well as northern territories of the municipalities of Kareli and Gori (area of 1,393km^2) have been under control of the authorities of the Republic of South Ossetia since 1992 and occupied by Russian troops since 2008 Russo-Georgian War.

Located in the central part of the lowland between Greater and Lesser Caucasus, Shida Kartli is bordered by the Russian Federation to the north, Mtskheta-Mtianeti to the east, Kvemo Kartli to the south, Samtskhe-Javakheti to the southwest, Imereti to the west, and Racha-Lechkhumi – Kvemo Svaneti to the northwest.

The relief of the region is comprised of extensive Shida Kartli plain and mountainous edges.

The population of Shida Kartli is about 259,300 according to the 2018 data. 94.7% of the whole population is Georgian, followed by 2.1% Azeris and 0.8% Armenians. The remaining percentage is divided among other ethnic minority groups.

- **Climate and Seasonality**

The climate in Shida Kartli is diverse:

- Moderate Humid Climate – the central part of the region, on the plain; to the north of the plain on southern slopes of the Greater Caucasus mountains and to the south on northern slopes of the Trialeti range; moderate cold winters and long warm summers.
- Transient climate from Dry Subtropical to Moderate Humid Subtropical – to the east from Gori environs, along Mtkvari valley; moderate cold winters and hot summers.
- Humid Climate – to the most northwestern part of the region, on western slopes of Likhi range and Racha range; cold winters and short summers (Humid highlands climate with lack of true summer).

Considering the information provided above, individuals can choose the suitable season to visit the region.

- **Religion and Language**

The majority of the population (96.5%) of Shida Kartli follows Orthodox Christianity while there are small groups of people following Islam. Along with that, approximately 3,500 people identified themselves as followers of other religions or no religion.

In the southern parts of Shida Kartli (the part which is under Georgian Control), people speak Georgian while some groups of people also speak Russian. In contrast to the south, in the north Ossetian is the language of the ethnic Ossetians, many of which also speak Russian.

- **How to get to Shida Kartli**

Take a minibus from Tbilisi. For further details visit the website below:
https://bit.ly/2nH6M35

- **Highlights of Shida Kartli**

- <u>**Uplistsikhe Cave Town**</u> – meaning the "Fortress of God" in English. It is an ancient rock-hewn city which played an essential role for Georgia for about 3,000 years. The artifacts that were excavated during archaeological research date back to the Late Bronze Age and all the way up to the late Middle Ages. To get to the cave, you can simply go on a one-day trip from Tbilisi. You can hire a local travel guide near the entrance of the cave to better understand the history of the place.

- <u>**Gori Fortress**</u> – historic fortress standing on a rocky hill in the center of the city of Gori. The ruins of the fortress indicate that there was a fortress dating back to the 1st century BC. Even though, the fortress was first mentioned in the Georgian historical manuscripts as "Gori Prison" only in the 13th century.

- <u>**Ioseb (Joseph) Stalin Museum**</u> – located in Gori, the museum was dedicated to the life of Stalin who was the leader of the Soviet Union born in the city of Gori.

In case if you are interested in Soviet-era characteristics, this museum is a perfect spot for you.

- **Accommodation**

Popular Hotels in Gori

Royal House
45 Samepo Str.
+995 599 90 91 29
https://bit.ly/2omYNsw
From 130 GEL

Old Gori
12 Tsereteli Str.
+995 599 51 70 62
https://bit.ly/2mH0H6X
From 100 GEL

Panorama
74 Rustaveli Ave.
+995 599 21 08 53
https://bit.ly/2m5qPYF
From 70 GEL

KVEMO KARTLI

- **Geography and Demographics**

Kvemo Kartli, which is considered as one of the most economically developed regions in Georgia, is a historical province and an administrative region in the southeastern part of the country.

The region comprises important municipalities, cities, towns, and villages, including Bolnisi, Gardabani, Dmanisi, Marneuli, Tetritskaro, Tsalka, and Rustavi. The regional capital of Kvemo Kartli is the city of Rustavi. Moreover, populated areas in Kvemo Kartli include 8 "dabas" which are the following: Didi Lilo, Kojori, Kazreti, Manglisi, Tamarisi, Shaumiani, Bediani, and Trialeti. Along with that, there are 338 populated villages in the region.

With the total area of 6,528km^2, the region is borders Tbilisi, Mtskheta-Mtianeti, and Shida Kartli to the north; Kakheti to the east; Samtskhe-Javakheti to the west; Armenia and Azerbaijan to the south.

The population of Kvemo Kartli is approximately 424,000, according to the 2017 data. 51.25% of the total population is Georgian (living mostly in the northern part of the region; Tetritskaro, Gardabani, Tsalka, Rustavi) while 41.75% is Azerbaijanis (living primarily in the southern part of the area; Marneuli, Dmanisi, Bolnisi). Moreover, 5.07% of the whole population is Armenian, 0.62% is Greek, and 0.49% is Russian. Armenians and Greeks mostly live in the northern part of Kvemo Kartli, specifically in the Tsalka Municipality.

• Climate and Seasonality

The weather during the early spring, late autumn, and winter months is quite cold and wet while summer months much warmer. For that reason, the best time for traveling to Kvemo Kartli is from late spring (more preferably even June) to early autumn (till the mid-September).

Due to the cold weather, the region is nearly unattractive and inconvenient to visit from November to March.

• Religion and Language

Taking into account the ethnic makeup of the total population, people living in Kvemo Kartli are from diverse religious backgrounds. The majority of the population (mostly Georgians, Russians, and Greeks) which is 57.8% identifies as Orthodox Christians followed by 38.9% Shia Muslims (mostly Azerbaijanians) and 2.8% Armenian Christians. The remaining percentage is divided among people with either no religion or other religious beliefs.

Majority of the population in Kvemo Kartli speaks Georgian while Azerbaijanian is also commonly spoken due to the ethnic makeup of the region. Considering the fact that Azerbaijanians have lived in the area for a long time, most of them can clearly speak and understand the Georgian language.

• How to get to Kvemo Kartli

Take a minibus from Tbilisi. For further details visit the website below:

https://bit.ly/2nH6M35

Moreover, to reach Rustavi, you can go to the Tbilisi Sports Palace (Sportis Sasakhle) and ask for the minibus to Rustavi.

- **Highlights of Kvemo Kartli**

The territory of the region comprises various remnants and tracks of all periods of mankind's history.

- **Rustavi Fortress** – an old discovered after the archaeological excavations in Rustavi. It is among the Georgian cultural heritages.

- **Dashbashi Canyons** – also referred to as Canyons of Tsalka. Located 110km away from Tbilisi and 2km away from the small town of Tsalka, it is considered to be one of the most fantastic travel destinations in Georgia. The surrounding area also features an important site, the ruins of medieval Kldekari Fortress.

- **Dmanisi** – an important archaeological site of the country. The area preserves one of the most interesting Paleolithic occupations of Eurasia as well as precious archaeological records of Georgia's medieval period. Dmanisi Museum-Reserve is open from late spring to early autumn (every day except Mondays). The museum offers guided tours in 4 languages, including Georgian, English, German, and Russian. For further details, you can follow the website below:
- www.dmanisi.ge

- **Accommodation**

Popular Hotels in Bolnisi

Guest House Bolnisi International
    38 Iakob Khutsesi Str.
    +995 596 10 50 10
    stumrissakhli@gmail.com
    From 100 GEL

Bolnisi Guest House
    10 Chavchavadze Str.
    +995 596 10 30 10
    N/A
    From 80 GEL

Popular Hotels in Dmanisi

Hotel Nabadi Dmanisi
    33b Tsminda Nino Str.
    +995 577 53 87 85
    https://www.facebook.com/hotelnabadi.dmanisi
    From 80 GEL

Apartament Dinara
    Tsminda Nino Str.
    N/A
    https://www.viamichelin.com/web/Hotel/Dmanisi-1700-_-
ef9580df
    From 70 GEL

. . .

Popular Hotels in Rustavi

Vejini
   N11 Rustavi, E60
   +995 595 55 51 72
   https://bit.ly/2nDdG9O
   From 160 GEL

Rustavi
   32 Megobroba Ave.
   +995 34 125 00 88
   https://bit.ly/2m5kTim
   From 100 GEL

Hotel Aquatopapa
   Rustavi, Automobile-Market
   +995 591 11 06 48
   https://bit.ly/2nDApm0
   From 100 GEL